Collected Poems

Also by E.J. Scovell

Shadows of Chrysanthemums
The Midsummer Meadow
The River Steamer
The Space Between
Listening to Collared Doves

E·J· SCOVELL

Collected Poems

CARCANET

First published in 1988 by
CARCANET PRESS LIMITED
208-212 Corn Exchange Buildings
Manchester M4 3BQ
and
198 Sixth Avenue
New York, NY 10013

PR
6037
C946
A17
1988

British Library Cataloguing in Publication Data

Scovell, E.J.
    Collected poems.
    I. Title
    821'.912   PR6069.C6/

    ISBN 0-85635-734-0

The publisher acknowledges financial assistance from
the Arts Council of Great Britain.

Typeset in 10pt Palatino by Bryan Williamson, Manchester
Printed in England by SRP Ltd, Exeter

Contents

5

V

VII LATER POEMS FROM *The Space Between*

Foreword

Many of these poems were first published in five selections: *Shadows of Chrysanthemums* and *The Midsummer Meadow* (Routledge, 1944 and 1946), *The River Steamer* (The Cresset Press, 1956), *The Space Between* (Secker and Warburg, 1982) and *Listening to Collared Doves* (The Mandeville Press, 1986). Several of the others, not published in book form, have been broadcast by the B.B.C. and a good many have appeared in periodicals and anthologies.

The third of the sections into which I have divided this collection is a series about babies and very young children. Apart from this the poems are not grouped by subject-matter but are on the whole, though not in detail, arranged chronologically, by time of writing not of publication; so that in all sections, except the last three, published and unpublished poems are mixed. Part VII consists of the later poems from *The Space Between*, Part VIII of those published in *Listening to Collared Doves*, and the last section contains uncollected work of the last few years. The translations of Pascoli were mainly done over a period when I was writing very little else, and so fit in with the chronological scheme.

Some earlier poems have been slightly revised.

I Early Poems

Light the Fire

Light the fire when night is near,
A little flame to span the night.
He will not feel the winds of fear
In the curved glades of fire-light.

And sing smoothly if you sing,
Lest he should hear between the stresses
The insensible cold rain falling
In unpeopled wildernesses.

With your song and vaulted light
Build his brittle starless ark.
With a curtain on the night
Overthrow the wild and dark.

The Sea Gull

All day, under me,
Foam burns of the sea.
Waves turn and bend for me
All day. All day
Dark or bright rains on me
Dust of sky and dust of sea.

That last wooden hoary stake
Where the farthest waves must break,
That is mine – to sit and see
Pastures turning under me,
Endless pastures, rich and live,
Where a bird may feast and thrive.

That is mine. There I see
All day, under me,
Waves turning of the sea;
All day, foam in flight
And noon curving into night.

Children Leaving a Wood

They came warily
Out of the dark trees.
Suddenly at their knees
The grass swung airily.

In the wood's fastness
The creepers clasp your waist;
You dare not speak nor haste.
But here is vastness.

In the wood's shadows
There are stops in life's beat.
Green brambles wound your feet.
Leaves freckle the sky's meadows.

(But they in pools of lightness
Shine downward through the thatch
And looking up you catch
Their wide resplendent brightness.)

In the wood, sound is fleeting.
They could be sure of nothing
But the leaves' sudden rustling
And their hearts strangely beating.

They came warily
Out of the trees' shadows
And saw the light sky meadows
And fields that airily

Swing with grasses hoary
Where the wind is never spent.
So they found their continent
And laughed and ran in glory.

After Reading All Day

When I have read till lights are lit inside
I shut my book up, thinking how I can
With few steps to the window open wide
The beauty of the evening like a fan;
How still in that light air the trees will grow
And lawns spread far and fall away from me.
Then I do open it, and even so
The lawns spread far, the trees breathe quietly,
And I go out (spoiling my opened fan,
Breaking the stillness of the evening)
And walk by the descending paths, and scan
The leaves of all the trees, imagining
They hold a poem my fain heart perceives.
But they are only the familiar leaves.

The Division

These small birds dart and stir
Safe through the steep tides of the days
And thread by secret ways
Through jewelled atoms of the air.

They are drowned as deep in life
As curling vortices or cloven
Ripples of water woven
Out of the tide's unresting strife.

They have eternity
Whom daylight holds too close to mark
There is another, dark;
Who hide from thought in curves of sea.

Like the still change of breath
Each timeless moment they are new,
And live life's whole life through
And die before they think of death.

Us their wide ocean mocks,
Our curbed and sequestrated wavès
That wind by sullen caves
And tortured furrows in the rocks.

For through this lucid day
Deep in the pale and tranquil sea
Small native birds make free
With the cool light and tilt and play.

But I am held apart
And only feel the slow waves beat
(Long flood and long retreat)
The rock partition of my heart.

Fragility of Dusk

The world is stretched so taut and thin
Before the pomps of night begin.
Rain in the air hangs caught like fire,
And every sound a narrow wire
Plucked by fingers out of sight;
And the sky empty, thinned of light;
And night falls crisply flake by flake.
The world is made of stuff so rare,
I think each moment it might break
To dust and vanish in the air
Or, seasoned wood, too dry, might leap
To sudden flame then fall asleep.

Past Time

You'll never understand *No Road This Way,*
But like a lost bird, on the window pane
Beating for skies, you'll throw yourself again
On the glass daylight of departed day.
For there seems open country: "There," you'll say
"The high streams flow between the sky and plain,

Between the hills so bright with hanging rain
The sky's thin atoms are less clear than they."
But light of yesterday is cold like glass.
Time that is past harder than diamond
Turns the fine air, and freezes to the bone.
The sap stirs once and slumbers when we pass.
The breath we breathe just thaws the air beyond,
Till stone we waked returns to harder stone.

Flowers

The first flower grows as high as the sunshine.
The second flower, more deeply planted,
Tilts up its muzzle yet, its serpentine
Light-seeking head, and body slanted.
And one curves deeply skirting by a stone,
And one flower rides the air upright.
These all look one way, as if a wind had blown,
And stretch one way, to grasp the light.

And in a dream I saw a flower that bent
From earth almost to earth its stem
And did not go the way the others went,
And yet was beautiful like them.

Lying Awake

"What have I to do with you?" Sleep said
To one who prayed her come, come to his bed.
"You have desired and lain with Consciousness instead."

21

To the Ruins by Night

When we came near the ruins I was afraid and lonely.
I told you so, but laughing, to disarm
Fear by a game of fear. You were young only
And might have mocked me, but you took my arm

And stumbling on twigs sprung low in the wet grass
And lost at times in undergrowth and shadows
You brought me to the open, to a star-lit space,
And we saw the abbey near, set in its meadows.

You were excited, shining like the sky,
But on my hand your hand was null and light.
Like a leaf I might be carrying I felt it lie
And might have dropped it like a leaf without thought in the night,

And dared not come, though you were set to show me
How quiet the aisles lay in the harmless air.
But I was afraid, because you did not know me,
That if I saw the ghosts you would not be there.

Marina

She has never come to the surface of the sea,
Never seen in daylight the world's proportions,
Ships in the crystal air and men at work on shore.

She walks on the sand of the sea bottom
Between the flowerless weeds; their branches, in number
Undetermined, in colour luminous,
Clutch and release her.

The keels of ships go over her like disaster;
She does not account for them. She makes nothing of the tides,
She is ignorant of the clouds and stars.

You think you speak to her but it is not she.
You think you are angry and she cries; it is not she who is crying.
She is walking on the many-coloured, unpeopled
Sand of the sea bottom.

The Sleeper

Love, your sleep's innocence became a weight in me,
And though you stand upright in sunlight, armed for day,
The pressure will not pass of your head turned away
And your sleep dropped like lead in my heart silently,

Of your sails furled, slipped to the deck; and called into
A narrow fold your life, shut into little space
Your sun and wind, and a stone pressed from all of you:
So burdens me your sleep, your undefended face.

Sand and Light

Every day that the sun sends
The flush will darken on the sands of pearl,
Every night till the world ends
At a known hour the known blue will flood all.

We who find the world is strange,
Come to each moment new as a new lover,
Who are trees to bud and change
Or men to traffic, sailing the seas over,

Their unchanging intercourse,
Day coming to the mineral earth, we never
Dream: for us is steadfastness
Forty years: a thousand years, for ever.

The Candle

Self-complete, unspoken
Single word of flame,
Clear as the unbroken,
The perfect word, the name:
If I try by breaking

Many words to make
Out of all one name
For this single flame,
Mine is not the same.

Love, you are your own speech,
You are a word once said
And lifted out of reach
Once in a language dead;
Formed like a crystal, one,
For ever said and done.
In vain with breath you buy
Life's multiplicity
To name that unity.

The Summer Evening

The sun is gone out, the day burnt down.
Now waxen and moth-white
The evening lifts to sight
A cold, extinguished candle's light.

Deep in this light, in this true hour
Is laid away
(In the wax the candle's ray)
All the inflammable substance of day.

It is for this the ox-eyed flowers,
Those that were sparse
In their groups peopling the long grass,
Now are a sea with skies held in their glass.

For this moths only, dense as clay,
And bats with falling flight
Pack the extreme twilight.
On this plumb-line earth drops in night.

London Children

The summer calls them from their holes.
They are creatures of no song,
But all the day their shrill and strong
Chattering is round the chestnut boles.

Their little flocks that wheel and cry
And twos and threes sprung everywhere
Up through the sun-muffled air
Are far as birds that know the sky.

They are boy and girl, and have names.
Their blood their own, their faces are
Distinct. They call from star to star
In constellations of their games.

What is assurance, what is found
Truth now and security,
But, moving in eternity,
The tight-rope challenge their limbs sound?

Birds Flying Home

Birds, swing eastward over the ocean-light.
Fly like leaves falling, drive and drift like snow.
Fly like an eastward falling, flakes of falling night,
Over the sky's, the earth's sea. Clouds and trees below
Riding at anchor lie each on its tide,
The sky and earth mirrors, the clouds and trees
Reflections, one in the other ratified.
Birds fall between the mirrors, between the seas.

Lucian

Subtle, cool, prim,
What do you mean?
What will you say
When the walls burn away?

Oh first and last
Sad and humorous
And strong in these,
Who will find your keys?

House undefended,
Fields untended,
Given up all goods
To the grass and the woods,

Losing easily
For hoarding's sake,
And giving carefully
For fear one should take –

Civilized,
Who will make you wise?
Who will find you, where,
Hidden in clear air?

The City Worker

In what I do, I speak.
I place my columns rightly.
Nothing I let unsightly,
Discordant, enter in.
So days lie in the week:
Sunday, the white margin.

Formal as church-attending,
Solved as hours of a nun,
From the hour of work begun
All the day's hours chime in order
Till the hour of work's ending:
Streets in drained light for a border.

Bird over Mountains

O green, most inland continent,
Should I rest and moor my ships,
Say "Stranger, quality of air,
Bird over mountains, feed from my lips"?

Music so solved is wild to me;
Morning I know, yet never meet.
Distance from me, strangeness to me,
Light on my wrist and eat.

Spring

All things are hidden
In their open being:
Trees in their flowering,
Fountains in showering,
Sight in seeing.

In a Cafe

Love, the bright tables bloom under lights
Under ground; the cloud-white ceiling low.
Far into distance, sown in order, blow
Wide the cloths, crocuses, aconites.
For your sake they are bright as snow;
For your long absence, changed to *immortelles*.
O flowers that sorrow has enamelled so,
Now even blind eyes would know you beautiful.

Soundless

City streets are so carpeted,
I am soundless.
If I weep a million eyes
Drink up my tears.

Or are they deflected into the sky
Along the branches of the plane trees?
Or changed to common light, like bird-song,
Or trodden into common dust?

No, they are borne away
By multitude, a drying wind.

The Suicide

Not daylight and not the dark,
Not even the outdoor evening, ebbing,
Yielded this woman her despair,
Her dead she sought, her drowned and still.
Daylight confuses with strong scent.
Darkness is an open door.
Evening is dense with words and tears.

With words we betray the vision.
Words with wind disturb the air,
With breath and eye-bright flicker of wings
Between our sight and still despair.
And tears breed pity, pity is
A tune, and music raises comfort,
The old, starved, elastic moon.

With her face reared, with her stone bows
She parted left and right through streets
The men like clouds. All things she saw
Her seeing mowed and bound in sheaves.
Yet she was quiet as a mouse
Or a small knife that makes its house,
Whose burrow is its own neat size.

And seeing all, she looked beyond
Famished to come to her despair,
And prayed in fear, in rage of will:
"Show me sorrow in still air.
For when I say I am betrayed
Wonder or pain confuses me,
Or a star falls and calls my eyes."

In still air, her own room was
Like an unlidded consciousness,
No light seen there, but a deep-sea,
Pearl-equal visibility.
In that pool she looked and saw,
Image of truth, the essence sorrow;
In that mirror ran to death.

The Boy Fishing

I am cold and alone,
On my tree-root sitting as still as stone.
The fish come to my net. I scorned the sun,
The voices on the road, and they have gone.
My eyes are buried in the cold pond, under
The cold, spread leaves; my thoughts are silver-wet.
I have ten stickleback, a half-day's plunder,
Safe in my jar. I shall have ten more yet.

Children's Names

Deep their obscurity,
Unchristened infancy,
Closed being, with no name;
Still, when a name is said,
They are flowers in darkness fed,
Nourished in the shadow of fame.

The names of children are
Name of a distant star,
Of a bird, sealed in green;
Given like a little boat
Vague over waves to float,
Drift light on worlds unseen.

Weak name that cannot bind
These hidden, undefined,
Even in deed not known.
Deeds of men burnish bright
Their name in mortal sight:
These escape, thistledown.

Leaves and Mortality

"Death is not from beyond us.
Not suns nor weather burned this tarnish on us.
The stamp of life could not be set upon us
Unless death's alloy bound us.
We never had drawn breath
In the air of time – we could not be"
(The leaves say, nickel-pale
At summer's end with inward death)
"But that we are compounded with the frail
Tough metal of mortality."

The Vain Girl Jilted

I can take cover
In good men's esteem,
In strangers' honour
From morning to night.

I can take cover
In the grace of being human
From the want of my lover
Who named me a woman.

All day I am clothed
From my head to my feet
In common kindness,
In courtesy;

All day my loathed
Flesh covered over
With favour of men –
That lost his favour.

At night I am naked.
I weep on my bed.
Night has no voice
But all is said.

Born Outcast

Born outcast or cast out young,
You famish to return, and lo,
Your feet and hands are home among
Your own; your face is seen to go
Between the native people to and fro.

Your house is in the settlement.
Your little slender tribe's good will
Under the sky first reared your tent –
Which has grown wings of stone, and cast them, till
You need a mountain palace for your pillow.

You need the honour of the stars. You know
You are so poor, you must have all: no less
Will staunch the lesion of the spirit flowing
Ever out into the wilderness
Where you have been, where you are, and are going.

Shunting of Trucks at Night

Shunting of trucks at night recalls me to
Far other wakeful nights, to breathe again
Their reed-thin air.
It was not sorrow nor anxiety
But a calm, subtle, flowering wakefulness:
Some wind had dropped that seed
Through intricate causes passing overhead.

And those long nights, threaded with the bell voices
Of the trucks one by one stayed on each other
By placid waterways,
Were featureless as upland plains, like them
Were hospitable to the traveller.
Even the light and air
Make themselves souls and entertain men there.

All night I travelled their outlandish ways
And fed on air, happy and not impatient,
Not fretful with slow time.
So the trucks play and will for me again
Always across clear space the cow-bell tune
They chimed at graze on those
Rare pastures where the grass was loved as flowers.

The New Year

It is more than we deserve, the turn of the year,
That comes in our sleep with so little stir.

We, ships that have passed our antipodes, stand
Thence with no change of course towards our native land

It is more than we deserve, it is more than we know,
The turn of our year that comes under snow.

The Giraffe

For neck, a tulip-stalk;
Flower-head, far off and elegant;
Tongue, to fill your body's want
Stretched out like hands of a lady
Who takes her own naturally;
Wind netted in your small-paced walk;

Eyes dark and innocent;
Airy beast with flower's grace,
With bird's speed, with human face;
Painted like ground under trees
With light and shade; supple as these;
Horizon's instrument:

Strength flowers, speed, in you.
Speed is your soul's obedience.
Tiger and strolling wolf must dance
To other tunes, obeying God.
Strength is their fruit, who feed on blood;
But the trees kneel for you.

O meshed among high leaves,
Among clouds: I should never start
To see, when clouds or branches part,
Like a wild cherub's, bloom your head,
Serpent wise, dove feathers spread
Brushing the poplar's sleeves.

A Winter Scene

This is heaven, the winter park they walk in,
Dissolution over, stars with leaves fallen,
The year corrupted away: it is full winter.

Father, child and mother walk in heaven,
Soberly in the mist, the tranquil heart
Of winter, arms linked or hands fallen coldly.

33

The ragged children are voices glancing on the trees
On the outskirts of heaven. They are heroic foot-prints
On the sodden steep slopes, the mouldered beech-leaves.

The lovers sway clasped hands, walk apart, are silent.
Like travellers on a frieze, like sojourners in heaven
They have forgotten even that they have forgotten.

In a Wood

I saw my love, younger than primroses,
Sleeping in a wood.
Why do I love best what sleep uncloses,
Sorrowful creaturehood?

Dark, labyrinthine with anxiety,
His face is like coiled infancy;
Like parched and wrinkled buds, the first of the year,
Thrown out on winter air.

Stiller than close eyes of a nested bird,
Clear from the covert of his sleeping,
One looked out that knows no human word
But gives me love and weeping.

Death from Cancer

Her face, though smaller than a child's, smaller than a flower,
Seemed forged in iron, or seemed quarried from granite,
Or carved in one stroke by lightning entering
The dense heart of a tree.

Her body had grown small as suddenly
And strangely as a dream dissolved in morning.
Crying through blankets, it seemed to those who had known her
    a woman
Not perished but returned to infancy.

And her skin was delicate and lustreless as woodsorrel,
As moths at dusk; but the east and age in its colour:
And not childhood, not lightness, not springing, but all
Close, compact substance was expressed in her.

Gentle and salt in life: black courage
Unwilled as the pain, and losing war without truce
Remained for her; for them visions of rock uncovered
By the tides of her comfort going down.

Bank Holiday: Primrose Hill

On this, the first Bank Holiday
Of the laborious year,
Such gentleness is manifest
In human shapes, in rainy air
Darkening – to make all clear
Man and woman need not speak.

But children's voices on the hill
Searching, answering, swing out far.
One, over space uncreated,
Hangs in the evening like a star,
Star-like rocket ripe for breaking –
Quenched now, swooping in what air?

Eyes at Night

Flowers quicken in the city night:
Their stillness, eyes' activity.
They seem beneath electric light
To look on all things equally
With bold and open innocence.

Eyes that receive and do not speak,
Of flowers, or children late awake;
Gates set too wide, to which worlds flow –
Who sifts that vast intelligence?
Who looks from you? Who sees? I know
In all that comes to thought or sense
The angel of the Judgement Day.

Swans

What do you carry in wings cupped so carefully,
Speaking of tenderness? *We carry life.*
Your neck well-nerved, easy and exquisite,
Whose is its immortal gesture of pride?
Not ours.
We in another world, further than stars,
Go on our own way. You need not hope to know
Whether our hidden feet enjoy their strength.

Whose pride joints your neck then, whose love curves your wings,
Who in my eyes consents?
The creeper rounds the stem and sees itself.
The god looks down upon his hands, two swans,
Asks what they are.

But now, beyond question, the swans sail on together,
Wing answering wing, as parting of a breath
Is close to its indrawing.
And the god in one sees himself in the other,
For his self-knowledge is the sailing of two swans.

But the swans do not know themselves possessed.
They go on their own way in their distant world.

II

The Canal

The canal lies through the city,
Half secretly, indifferently,
Visible and from strangeness invisible.
On other levels, in other worlds

The streets are. Here between the road bridge
Walled breast-high, and railway bridge,
A little shadowed length lies
Of well-deep water bare to sky.

And from one bridge's dark to the other
An empty barge with bright coal-dust lined
Slides smoothly like a fish, silently is
Under the day's eye and his who sees:

As lives of children and thoughts of men glide
In darkness, in the deep, and are on the wave
Lit for moments unannounced,
And those who are there may see.

The Museum Lights Reflected in a Picture

The ancient picture's glass receives
The moon-round, unlustrous lights.
In its dark silk and silent streams
They are naturalised and dwell.

The admirable geese with naked eyes,
Transparent, grown like water, hold
Moons in their body as pearls. They give
To those who ask them who they are, the moon,
And hide within the moon.

All the late afternoon, eyes sound
The picture and can touch no rock –
Hidden from eyes in light, from thought
In simplicity and speechless age.
The birds like strong tenacious ghosts
Live on and say no word.

The Swan's Feet

Who is this whose feet
Close on the water,
Like muscled leaves darker than ivy
Blown back and curved by unwearying wind?
They, that thrust back the water,
Softly crumple now and close, stream in his wake.

These dank weeds are also
Part and plumage of the magnolia-flowering swan.
He puts forth these too –
Leaves of ridged and bitter ivy
Sooted in towns, coal-bright with rain.

He is not moved by winds in air
Like the vain boats on the lake.
Lest you think him too a flower of parchment,
Scentless magnolia,
See his living feet under the water fanning.
In the leaves' self blows the efficient wind
That opens and bends closed those leaves.

A Child Crying

His tears rose far away but here they must fall,
Here on earth drain to the asphalt path
From his wet hands, or with slow pains crawl
Through rusted chinks of the toy car.

The elder boy struck him in angry play;
But he gives no account of tears
That rose in rocks and mountains far away.
Like a speechless baby, his

Pain is incommunicable. The world's
Contours guided it down to this hour.
It knows no cause nor name; its face
Is turned on him, away from us.

A Field

The field is bounded by four hedges built of may
Like stone. There, seen or unseen, the blossom is given,
Jets out from the deep springs of time all day;
Gone, is replenished. The scent floods for its season.

The grass in the square field is thin as wire, as dew;
Erect each grass, tarnished like colour under the moon,
With roseate mist, a fire-reflecting smoke, run through.

The short and brittle-seeming, cloudy grass
Peoples this framed and empty field as souls do heaven,
That travellers stare from the gate and cannot pass.

The Ghosts

The days of our ghosthood were these:
When we were children, when we had no keys
We entered through closed doors, unseen went out again.
Our souls were the dissolved, ungathered, filtering rain.
Our bodies sat upon our parents' knees.

In the second days of our ghosthood
We went on foot among a multitude,
In time of drought, in our hard youth, we winter-born.
And those were visible to men as flowers in corn
Whose souls were eyes unseen that gaze from dark.

We entered flesh and took our veil, our state.
The third days of our ghosthood wait.
When we are stripped by pain, by coming death far-seen
Of earthly loves, earth's fruit, that came so late to hand,
With that waking or falling into dream
We shall not cross into an unfamiliar land.

Bloody Cranesbill on the Dunes

We saw one first and thought it was the only one
For beauty made this flower seem to be alone
As stars burn each alone in gulfs of time and space.
And opening distance like a star, with sunset face
Broken through earth as angels part the clouds, it made appear
The grass a firmament, confusing far and near.

As the evening star was not and is suddenly
On the fresh lawn of heaven, the clear, unbroken sea –
Not made with hands, nor born, it shines, not says "I am" –
So the one flower seemed in the grass, the shell-heart flame.

But the night ripens and another star
Takes body where none seemed in the ghost-laden air;
And summoned to men's sight, exorcized to lay down
Invisibility, they crowd our vision,
Thicker than birds or bees, than clover leaves or stones;
And hands of children gather these solitary ones.

For most alone is most accompanied.
I watched the ballet dancer's lonely, floating steps and head
Proud, meek as one unborn, and wondering saw that she
Was compassed with her solitary kind, a galaxy.

So walking through the dunes the second day, we found
Another cranesbill flower, a world sprung from the ground;
And there a third and fourth, and further on the source,
The blood-tipped seeds, the opened rosy flowers,
There risen in time, a freshet flooding; strange and hard to see
As if they had been always known, yet could not be.

Ash Trees

The ash trees grow like fountains
With pliant jets, arched and descending,
And leaves of water many-fingered,
Now by autumn rarefied.

They are blown back upon themselves in wind
Like fountains, and blown wide,
And lose some substance in the air
Beyond their fountain-bowl and sphere,
But most call in, call home.

But where the lost goes no thought follows,
The leaves, the invisible foam struck separate as worlds in air,
In autumn when the substance rends and loosens
And the spirit is pouring everywhere.

A Madman

Two in the abstract dark talk all life long.
Hear through the thin partition voice and counter-voice,
Closer than speech of angels over the light-years.

It is the argument of one with one.
The days pour in and pass: these are set to their night,
As lovers to their night and equilibrium.

A Stranger

I saw a woman drag her foot,
Inept pass through the day,
As if she had an idiot child
Who bled her life away;

As if her ghost stayed in a room
High under roofs, that none
Could see inside; there nursed a fire
That never must burn down.

There like a piled fire intense
Or tree fed by her will,
One lived, unique, a gulf of life
Her life flowed out to fill.

The running children in poor streets
Grazed with their eyes her own.
Far in the mountains of her heart
The infertile streams poured down.

Whom all could wound, yet none could touch,
What child or thought or soul,
Terror or pain she tended there
Her passing did not tell.

A City Park in Winter

Now men like trees walk through the world,
Columns of fire. The trees like men
Hold out their budding hands to heaven,
Laden and bruised within with spring.

Compact and crocus-coloured gulls,
Neat on the grass in ranks like city flowers
Or flowering shear from rock-like water,
Say: "We are beads of fire."

Pearls of fire, with folded wings,
In separation and integrity
Nursing the fountains of their blood;
Spreading their wings like winds of fire.

And the young swans hooded in dun
With their feet like washed lotus leaves
Say: "We are formed to bear with grace those rippling seas,
Lapping of life within against the shell."

Through the visible, like smoke piled and thin,
The wands and roots of fire almost break to sight,
Outline, fill out with flame these blanched, fog-coloured ones,
Declare themselves in them, as in the ripened sun.

An Old Land

Sometimes the mist parts and
The country of your mind appears:
The slow-sloped stubborn hills
And, guessed between, the ferny woods
Like the small shadows in the throats of flowers;

Faithful rocks, and lower
The breathing fields that pray to light;
Few flowers, and some strange, imported,
Run wild. It is an old land, crossed and ploughed and haunted,
And the new year, the present, the eternal,
Lies deep on it like dew.

The Hospital Room

In this green room the flowers stand
As though upon their earth.
Their look is like intelligence,
The light-receiving moon.

Though the blind drawn, I know beyond
Four blackened, combed poplars
Before a shut-faced house converse
With wind and chimney-stacks,

Both now and in slate morning light –
When beautiful and shamed,
Like the late-walking cat, dawn creeps
Through city forests home.

I know it's turning the corner
When the first brooms are out,
Mats shaken, and the nurse with head
Averted counts the pulse.

But now is evening, and the city
Poplars, night-wise dawn
Vanished; absence' self shut out.
A shielded lamp and flowers

Set all on fire; but not as fires
Of coal make the room flame.
This burns with incandescent light
Like harvests praising sun.

From the Hospital Window

The pigeons know their way
Tumbling in seas of wind.
The poplars stream like corn.
The fruit-like heavy birds
Launch out and are up-borne,
Or weight the high roof's rails.
Wind warps their seaward feathers.

The trees let loose their twigs –
Struck far as meteors.
The osier-pliant stem
Weaves the air's will, and swings
Ever slow-settling to its north,
Its native poise again.

The Clean Pillow-Case

They gave me a clean alpine pillow-case
And bathed my eyes with snow.
I thought I would not wish for happiness,
For vital joy and energy again –
Release from pain so bears
Its own uncoloured, mountain-scented flowers.

Pain was almost my friend, my hands, my groove,
My part of winter's day.
All the joy I could bear, all I could love
Was innocence and lightness of pain gone,
And in the window's frame
The white air present as a face and name.

Evening on Primrose Hill

Late, the evening light diffused
Whitens planes and facets of
This tossed sea-surface of the grass.

Where lovers have left one form
And where feet have ploughed and harrowed;
Where the sun lay slack like water;

The millions of the grass
Loosen and breathe invisibly. The evening
Whitens their sides with dust of silver sand.

The people of the grass, that have
Bowed to this summer and this human day,
Transfigured shine, like men or nations

That have endured the flooding of
Time or sorrow or philosophy,
And are lustred by knowledge like a bloom.

Alone

Nothing will fill the salt caves our youth wore:
Happiness later nor a house with corn
Ripe to its walls and open door.
We filtered through to sky and flowed into
A pit full of stars; so we are each alone.
Even in this being alone I meet with you.

Ordinary Death

What is death to the dead? to us a fountain,
Greenness, a salt preservative;
Wind blowing for imagination
And blood-desired food of all who live;
Breath, necessity, companion;
Terror purging our casual corruption.

But to the dead, is death not known, or wholly,
Or still half known, remote and near?
When the confused and mediocre
Die, whose unheroic lives were dear,
Trouble them not with strange intensity.
Be to them as in life, and let them be.

The Island in the Park

The seven-masted island
At rest in the wrought lake
Flies in my mind a swan.

Spaces between the poplars,
White flags of winter sky,
Are its sails, are its wings.

Though the evening dogwood
Touches the water's face
(Polished like precious stone);

Though stags with emblem antlers,
Reared softly among oaks,
Drink from that chiselled bowl;

Still the prowed and masted island
Winged with white space of sky
Flies like a wild, sea-dwelling swan.

Flames

See the flames behind the bars,
Flowers sheltered in a garden, tended phlox,
Small and soft the air caressing,
Caressed, like blades of grass rooted among damp rocks;

Yet wild, in their limbs life expressed:
Though they, the wind or human will obeying,
In a narrow range curvet,
It is life cracks them each like whips, like banners baying.

Flowers with stillness of their race,
The tamed hours of the day, we did not tame,
Love that wills to come to hand –
It is flame holds their heads; our earth and blood are flame.

Praise them then for courtesy.
They veil themselves for us, subdue their power,
Give for rage, docility,
Moss-rooted grass for fire; the flower hides in the flower.

See the flames behind the bars,
Flowers sheltered in a garden, tended phlox,
Small and soft the air caressing,
Caressed, like blades of grass rooted among damp rocks.

Like Breath

Though you enter me like breath
Or like the spaces set between
The atoms of my bone,
And move in me, to both unknown,
Thinner than water, when I am alone;

Though you, walking in your sleep,
Divide my substance like a sea
And part my thoughts and pass
Through walls and thorny forests free –
Your waking soul has not the master key.

Happiness

Like the blue sea joined around
My land, the sea-blue air
I breathe; like slow forests, feet
And hands of trees clasping the rocks
On mountains, the trees blue-dark all the year;

Like earth and water where they change
On shallow coasts (the sea
Now at my door, now full convex
Shadowing my marsh meadows; now
The long beach scrolled with sand and purple weed);

Like all things present, like nightfall:
Outside, the mind's release,
World thread-drawn, whiteness through the fabric
Showing: indoors, darkening, fire, pause,
And comfort known, like a child held on knee.

A Room at Nightfall

As England's earth moves into dark, the fire is painted,
Shines like speech in the dulled room.
Nocturnal lights of man come out in streets and windows
And cars heard passing. Last to bloom
Of all lights, the narcissus-white lamp on our table
Flowers at a touch, is shaken wide;
And far the sky, Euridice, falls back, the house-roofs,
Night trees are emptied. We inside
Seem to hang in a domed pearl where light with shadow,
Shadow is interfused with light.
Draw the curtains, perfect the moon-round, moon-coloured
Globe that hangs so still in night.

A Betrothal

Put your hand on my heart, say that you love me as
The woods upon the hills cleave to the hills' contours.

I will uphold you, trunk and shoot and flowering sheaf,
And I will hold you, root and fruit and fallen leaf.

Marriage and Death

We are not dovetailed but opened to each other
So that our edges blur, and to and fro
A little wind-borne trade plies, filtering over,
Bartering our atoms when fair breezes blow.

Though, not like waters met and inter-running,
Our peoples dwell each under different sky,
Here at high, unsurveyed, dissolving frontiers
We cannot prove: "This is you, this is I."

Oh now in you, no more in myself only
And God, I partly live, and seem to have died,
So given up, entered and entering wholly
(To cross the threshold is to be inside),

And wonder if at last, each through each far dispersed,
We shall die easily who loved this dying first.

Love's Immaturity

Not weaned yet, without comprehension loving,
We feed at breasts of love; like a still cat
That wears and loves the fire in peace, till moving
She slips off fire and love, to cross the mat

As new as birth; so by default denying
House-roof and human friends that come and go,
The landscape of life's dream. Antelopes flying
Over his wild earth serve the lion so.

We are blind children who answer with love
A warmth and sweetness. Those even we love most
We sleep within their lives like cats, and rove
Out in the night, and late return and coast

Their souls like furniture. Oh, life should give
Light till we understand they live, they live.

The Poor Mother

"Hush!" she says by rote under the trees
On park seats, with one hand moving the pram.
She holds a child like fate upon her knees
On long train journeys, in the sleepless tram,

Like a part of her body, like her heart.
She seems half numbed and lost to him, her care,
But her dull touch and words, the kind or tart,
Indifferent, move in his sighing breast like air.

And she waits long with her sick children in
Hospital corridors and ante-rooms;
Till the door opens and the rites begin,
Talking with other women low among tombs;

And late goes where deepest his shadow lies
Who is her friend and enemy and lover –
Lies over earth and over her and these
The children that he took and carved out of her.

Orchids in a Drought

Wild purple orchids here and there
An inch high in the short grass stood,
As dense with light as precious stones,
As strange on earth as drops of blood:

Stones that have poured and poured their close
Packed colour endless years through earth;
Blood that, deeply lodged in flesh,
Fearful and lustrous comes to birth.

By a dry ditch the dock and rushes,
The buttercup and cowslip head
Hardly looked out over the starved world's roof-top.
Here a deep vein was pricked and bled.

Summer Beeches

The foreheads of the beeches,
The elephant-calm brows,
The day touching whitens,
Clouded, open-palmed:

More single than stone mountains,
Stiller than cows and sheep;
By summer weighted, anchored,
Full-leaved to the long grass.

But closer, but more distant,
See the curled outmost shoots
That high and uncontrollable
Weave like fire or sea waves,

And break on air, their shore,
With endless subtle sounding.
That white the light picks out,
It is a wild sea's foam;

And through its changing mazes,
Like fish in coral seas,
Like thought in a brain's winding,
Thread lives of blackbirds, doves.

Change

He is younger than us all
And will live to a later day,
And our intentions he will change.
See, they are changed: he branches clear away.

What our thought would do falls dead,
As the clenched dreamer's body lies
In impotence of dreams like stone.
Where we sowed corn, flowers sunrise.

Our children, even our changeling deeds,
Dwell in a land where God disposes.
"I have loaves in my basket" said the saint.
"Open your basket." They had turned to roses.

Fishing Villages on the Labrador Coast

Like cowrie shells or seeds,
The few and worthless beads
Spaced wide by knotted twist
On a child's neck or wrist,
One on a stone door-step
Sitting alone between
All earth outside and in –

On the gulf's shore, so sparse,
White huts strung on the grass
Thinly and poorly gem
The savage inland's hem,
As if one only played
The rich domains of man,
His treasures here began.

But this is a true door-stone,
Threshold of known, unknown.
Outposts of each in each
The huts shine on the beach.
The fishers at their trade
Seem the clear shadows cast
Of worlds unseen and vast.

Up the River

That morning when I woke and stretched from sleep a hand
I touched a country far inland.
The ship come to the wide river from seas by night,
Like a barge laden, like insight
Threading that sleeping heart, bared the deep-wooded strand.

There like a crystal dream, a drawing on a page,
A scene set forward on a stage,
Like flowers or fruit on a girl's apron when she lifts
And holds it spread, to offer gifts –
Stiller than these, a wave-bound church and white village.

A World of Glass

In a charmed light, blue without source or shade,
In a shop window a world of glass was made,
With glass giraffes to feed from antlered trees
And glass ships sailing the locked waves of seas.

Too brittle for children's play, not made to endure,
Too chic to be beloved more than a year;
Creatures of poise too conscious, over-stressed
In the blind diamond light, boat, pavilion, beast.

The city's cold electric fires are pain
To hold the night awake and force man's brain
Like spring that would be coiled, from self apart.
Of all the city this glass world is heart.

World spoiled before born; yet it in its own sun's light shines,
Light somewhere created, streaming new from mines;
And these, unpriced as stars falling on nights of frost,
Live far from us their obscure life till life is lost.

A Flint

Darker than lakes in whose heart light
Deepens darkness, light fallen
Not to return but as a voice
Of ghost from catacombs,

The polished, dark-translucent flint,
Receiving earth and time,
Gives back no gleam to mortal eyes
But holds and hoards its known;

Heavy with long endurance, ribbed
By pressure like sea-sand;
By tidal earth, by seasons, men,
Worn like the haft-shaped hills.

Mid-Winter Flowers

Flowers brought out of darkness, white or bruised with shade,
Jonquils and Roman hyacinths, freesias with grassy leaves,
Show the end of the year in curtained English rooms.

As white as Christmas cakes, as frost on fir and yew,
They lean through windows to the sky's unlighted plains of snow,
The winter-patient gables in the nets of trees.

But when lights are lit they dress themselves freshly.
Like faint sea-weed that crisps and dances in the risen tide,
In air of lamp-light these preen and glow, colourless.

On the oak table, earth-islanded in their bowl,
Or stilled, a fountain, in their vase, they tell our year's midnight
And turn our thoughts to east with scent and cold of dawn.

A Head

His fruit-shaped head is a vessel made to hold
Knowledge like fruit; and hold in poise the whole
Labyrinth world, like coiled eternity
Painted in some clay mortal-purposed bowl.

His eyes set in their beautiful declines
Seem arcs of lustrous-aired invisible skies.
They pray for knowledge and for innocence,
Gazing like children's eyes, but serpent wise.

A Wife

Beloved, a year has gone
Whose time seemed still as water of canals.
I am not used to the house linen yet,
The sheets still folded clouds; your china still
On the top shelf shows faces new to me;
And I am still a stranger and
The youngest in your house.

I was born here a second time, to learn
Slowly like a child, by heart and touch,
Till your life's web and furnishing
Grows older in me than my cradle, rooms
Never unknown; till your traits sound
Deeper in me than my inheritance
From childhood and my parents' unplacated genes.

I have drunk forgetfulness
Of former worlds: this is my sole one. Strange
Is to a child one with familiar; but his hands
Dream floating, then are clumsy as they learn
To hold a spoon and button shoes.
Like a long-sleeping child, half by passivity
I learn your substance and soul's reach
As coasts must learn the sea.

The Owl

All night the hunting owls
Above suburban lawns
Answered each other's oboe voices.
O dedicated, limpid wildness!

One stayed self-echoing late
In mindless genius free
When the night was lifted somewhat,
Stretched high and vague above the city,

And day had drawn back far
To spring, fall in song-foam,
Though no birds of day sang yet.
The owl called on and on alone,

All space its sheath and ear;
Then ceased and nothing was.
Suddenly – what wild valley crossed? –
A blackbird's voice of friend spoke near.

Time for Sleeping

Do not look up. I will turn away soon.
The light is trained down on your book; your head
Shows lit yet, incandescent as the moon
Seems. What is still between us is not dead;

It sleeps and draws far in itself in dreams.
My thought and gazing, like a willow leaf,
Shallowly comb that deep; the surface gleams
Frayed now. My greedy consciousness and grief

Confused and anxious cry to love to wake,
To know itself each hour because life flies.
I think of war and death. You, for life's sake,
In our love's time for sleeping do not raise your eyes.

The Flame's Life

In being and not-being
Flame has its life, on air
Printed, and gone; a moment
Its shape stands where it was.
Our eyes clutch late like children
Touched in a blindfold game.

Now born again it follows
Through space its varied, one
Journey and theme; in motion
Wild and leashed, like a leaf
Blown on its tree, or circling
Marionette on string.

As we have sleep and waking
And mind knows death in sleep,
This leaves its form, re-enters,
Sits like a ghost at board,
And slips to dark as glibly
As we to our dark sleep.

Day and Night

My life drains down to sleep.
The dayward slopes are dry and wear
A desert beauty only,
Unploughed and full of air,
And the air full of light, and colour unborn.

There the short grasses vowed
To poverty and namelessness
Make themselves into seas to mirror sky,
And wide-spaced sheep feed on the grass,
And seem grown thin, fed on eternity.

But the dark slopes tax
My dole of life with storms and streams.
Adult-born rivers spring from the divide
Of falling asleep, and breed rankness of dreams,
Hang the exhausting creepers in the glades.

And voices sip my blood.
It is my dream-selves and their friends
Using my life because they must
For their strong, trivial ends,
To throw me out on morning bleached and drowned.

III   *Poems on Infancy*

The First Year

I

All deeds undone, all words unsaid,
Null as a flower, sleep on my bed.
None to compare you with, for you
Are type and inmost form of New.

Darkness your home – what need at all
To be cast out, washed, wrapped in shawl;
And soon, the same yet not the same,
Be bent to attributes and name?

What should you do, new born, but fall
Asleep, in sleep disclosing all?
What can you do but sleep, an hour from birth,
Lacking an answer yet to give to earth?

II

Before she first had smiled or looked with calm
Light-answering eyes and claimed to be of man
I put my finger in her shadowy palm,
And her own whispering ones from their chestnut fan
Closed again (as they must) on mine, to a bud.
Then I was where strong currents piled and slackened.
Like a pulse telling all the power of blood
This palm seemed the cavern where alone her darkened
And secret rock-roofed river showed to man
(Except when one inside half-raised the blind
Of her inky eyes, and fierce a dark beam ran
Searchlighting day). So I strayed on her mind;
And thought I trespassed in that covered land.
Her hand seemed private, still an unborn hand.

III

In what dignity she lies
Resting on her world
Her unjudging, cloudless eyes;

Making helplessness protection;
Making immaturity
(So full she fills her state) perfection.

Perfectly, without room for more or less,
Her unskilled body arches to express
To a known face coming, joy and friendliness.

IV

Is it then an imaginary world
Where I speak to my baby in English words,
And half believe she understands my tongue
Like the young of animals and birds;
Half think we play a game she understands,
And she laughs at being a child, weak in my hands?

V

As monks whose time is told by bells
Out of their strict hours see eternity,
I have watched your eternity, your world without beginning,
These five months by the moon;

These days by the clock with their ritual repetitions,
Votive milk and early rising,
Plains of peace and fainting terrors,
And their meaning out of time.

For between one feed and another,
Your sleep's forgetting, your calms of waking
Have freed me to eternity
Like the sky through a little window-frame.

VI

I am absorbed and clouded by a sensual love
Of one whose soul is sense and flesh the substance of
Her spirit; and her thoughts, like grass shadowed by the wind's
    flight,
Her hands' bemused and under-water dance in light.

Will, waked in lashing limbs, drops in her like a flame.
Her love is parting of lips to suck or smile (whose birth the same);
Her excreting, her lonely task; her communication,
Her body arched for hands to hold, harp-strung with jubilation.

When I serve her (whose sense is soul) I serve her all,
Whose feeding is her love, whose mind in bone grows tall;
And watching her (whose thoughts move without words like
    wind on grass)
I am less than I was my own; I am not what I was.

VII

The days fail: night broods over afternoon:
And at my child's first drink beyond the night
Her skin is silver in the early light.
Sweet the grey morning and the raiders gone.

VIII

The baby in her blue night-jacket, propped on hands
With head raised, coming out to day, has half-way sloughed
The bed-clothes, as a sea-lion, as a mermaid
Half sloughs the sea, rooted in sea, basking on strands.

Like a gentle coastal creature she looks round
At one who comes and goes the far side of her bars;
Firm in her place and lapped by blankets; here like tides
Familiar rise and fall our care for her, our sounds.

IX

Whom do I know? Who learns from me to kiss, to play?
Who answers sound with sound and looks with eyes of friend?
Strange that this long first year of life, this standing day
In which you are set like stone in ring, in which we meet, will
    more than end;

Will drop far out of sight, and you become another,
Sister and stranger to this self, changed without motion,
Caught in acquirements, calling things names, calling me mother;
But lost this lucid year, dropped out of sight, this key dropped
    in the ocean.

X

The child looks out and away: to the woman's maternal-bound
Thought away raying from her, light-reined; but chiefly
She looks away from herself, when on the floor she briefly
With all the moment's life examines a hair-pin found
Or a knot in the board; or when her fingers spell
(Whose gestures are diffident and tender) – touch and trace,
As if they searched there for the features of a face,
The carpet's pattern, never seen before so well.

It does not surprise the baby that she is a human
Soul already, established citizen of earth;
She takes her life and state for granted, teased the most
By little concrete things; but it surprises the woman,
Still seeing her face, formed and reserved, the day of birth,
And the perils and the spaces of her voyage to this green coast.

XI

When the old sleep, a sadness moves beholders;
And when the strong mature, whose shoulders
Support the world in their generation's hour –
Strangely sleep's weakness lies with power;
But when you sleep, sleep only seems your other
Self, your flower's leaf, your brother.

Sleep's unknowing, where so little's known,
Is a lamb with a lamb lying down.
And sleep's imprudence and unguarded nature
You wear like any thornless creature,
Open, upturned to dangerous nights and days
Like scabious where the cattle graze.

Not fast like ours your categories seem;
Your dreams play with your waking dream.
And bold all visions come into your net –
The rage of thought not on you yet,
That frightens the many to a standing stone
So it may seize and have the one.

Not at the pillow end of your big bed
You sleep, but where your wandering head
Happens to tire and rest. So sometimes, thrown
Far out on your blue eiderdown,
You seem a sleeping sea-bird, guarded best
By yielding to the sea, wild sea its friend and nest.

Gestures

Last summer cradle-bound, to whom the world must come,
Must wait with gifts for her at the gates of sleep, her home,
Now come herself out to the world, she grasps and stands,
And will print it with her feet and change it with her hands.

But though she trains her novice limbs morning to night
Those hands and feet seem still not for use but delight –
Such movements in their stumbling open, shine, fade like flowers,
Gestures that seem the words of an older world than ours,

Pristine gestures that seem led down, and no drop spilt,
From man's first speech of dance before the Tower was built;
And fresh, archaic, springs – here low by conduit led
From mountains – her erect and tendrilled human head.

Dreams

I can guess your dreams now
But this I cannot guess:
What you dreamed an hour from birth;
What is paid for consciousness;
What you have unlearned, to learn
Competence of earth.

Heavy as Lead

I

For our children are the children of our flesh
And the body of our love. The love that was
Before child-birth seems airy, feathery,
Frond-like now, a spirit moving grass.

Lovers' love which is a spirit must take
Flesh, the bodies we beget and bear;
And flesh is heavy and opaque
And a lodestone to care.

II

Heavy as lead, heavy as water
That seeks with obdurate art
And finds for resting-place the deepest part,
So heavy in us is our tender daughter.

Heavy in us – to God or stranger
A spirit or leaf-light sapling,
To us she is a leaden anchor grappling
To sand and central rock; the ocean-ranger

Strains against it. Heavy as earth
On a tree's roots when the green tree,
Its sunward frame, is racing like a sea.
So heavy is child-love, and holds us as if she,
Our child, were ground that gave us birth.

A Voice

The child is slow to speak in words
But makes, as sometimes birds
Or water flowing deep in ground,
A human voice's sound –
Only that theirs could never seem
(The speech of bird or stream
That startles first with likeness, then proves different)
Perfectly human like her speaking, and intelligent.

Foreign voices please the ear
When suddenly we hear
Without the office of the mind
The mere note of our kind.
But hers, that has meaning for none
But lives as sound alone,
Quick, limpid, gentle, seems the soul, distilled from sense,
Of what is human most in man, his tongue's intelligence.

A Moment

The apple blossom, the sensuous infant charm;
The human rounded arm
Dipping to the elbow, with that slight scythe-twist,
The forearm's swerve to wrist;

The bibs and pots and the elaborate care
Round her continuous as air;
Her time of life with all its dress, with its cloud-scapes
Muffling the sky in gleams and shapes;

Her childhood and its circumstance fell far away
Then as she turned from window-play
With a fledged, conscious look. It seemed a bird stretching,
Seven feet from wing to wing.

A Sleeping Child

Her toys, the three small battered wooden elephants,
Lie below her pillow in the crook of shoulder and head.
Pushed down, the covers lap her arms – from her joined hands
Flow round her, following the arms' curve up the bed.

She on her back, framed by the pillow and clothes' arc,
By her position's symmetry, composed by night,
In daylight never still, now in the almost dark
Gloom through the door, arrests like a hand raised, like a light.

By what authority? She wields in sleep three mysteries:
First, her own still mute nature; secondly, sleep's secretness;
Visible beauty like a third darkness laid over these,
Like speech of gods, whose words are lost on earth in clap of voice.

Embroidery

Child, when I swing you up and down
You make a chevron pattern travelling over time
Like the embroidered zigzag stitch I use to seam
The shallow yoke of your nightgown;
And when I walk along lifting and lowering you,
On the walls and the air you make this pattern too.

You are the adornment of our days,
Your life so pattern-regular, your looks so pretty
They seem a golden thread embroidered on our city;
And your impelled and formal ways,
Not rational to us, obeying foreign laws,
We think them fair designs yet do not know the cause.

You speak to heart and eyes, a tongue
Baffling thought that jibs at the knowledge in your smile,
Your adult certainty of choice, with all the while
Child-charm, as though small bells were hung
To sound on hair and wrists and ankles as you moved
And make you beautiful to us, so make you loved.

With Flowers of Grass

My frisky flower, erratic flickering mover,
Butterfly on the silver grass's head,
I see you not far branched from sorrel and clover.
Now while the flowers of earth seem a light shed,
Not her own but a gilding, a heavenly rain,
You shine with the other beams and dance in their train.

And it is peace to see you so, for I
Still in my sleep dress, feed you, and feel printed
The shape of your head on my bones of hand and thigh
(Where you run to crouch in fear the ground is dinted).
For peace I gather your simple flowering look
With flowers of grass, and press them in a book.

New-Born Sleep

The gradual dove-grey shadow lies
Deep in the valleys that rim his sleeping eyes.

Cradled from lamp and fire – what moon's
Light is upon those undiscovered dunes?

Before Milk

Image of concentration,
Silver vase of expectation –
Hunger is holy, stripped so bare
In your face narrowed to a star
And sweet black suckling stare,
Now when your lips, though mute
After crying, seem pursed to flute,

Or poised, a flower-bud,
To break into their good,
Their crown and flower of satisfaction;
To spring from carved and soundless waiting
Into the song of their perfection,
Which can give your soul ease
And sleep of foam dispersed on seas.

A Boy of Four Months

In his first flowering, in the prime and pause,
The summer of his infancy,
The dark-blond boy on the strange bed alone
Lies like a rosy stone cast by the sea.

He is as self-sufficient as the stone,
Rounded with milk; and like the air
Or like a dream, a waking calm well-being
Laps him and folds and enters everywhere.

In the simplicity of his receiving
Our world – our feeding, tending and leaving
And looming again (he opens like a flower
To a smile on the bed) – there strongest sleeps his power.

A Protest

When I am hungry I must cry.
Do not be misled
By all my conscious airs or by
My head shaped like my father's head,
Or by the expert language of my laughter.
Do not be beguiled
To think I am all essence and hereafter.
I am a six-months child.

Child and Baby

It is the long brows like wings
That brood her sleeping face. Still
Lips and cheeks are infantile;
The future curves her brow –

A child already so committed
To life and compromised so,
Come so far, so far to go
That she seems sleeping now

Dropped in her path, on the world's rim;
More in her heart's complexities alone
(Passions and toys, flowers, thickets of thorn,
All her life's symbols taken root and sprung) –

More lonely than the baby, who has learnt
No skill to dazzle nor dividing word;
Whom we say "sweet" to, like a bird,
In speech as clear as song.

A Baby's Head

The lamp shines on his innocent wild head again.
Only for a moment are you both flowers and men,
Your souls like souls of flowers wholly immanent;
Your soul a texture and your love a scent.

In fifty years if you have beauty it will be
Words written on your face, abstract as history.
The light will call you foreign with its sharp and changed
Glancing, among earth's aspects call you strange.

Now even the captive light still in a sheltered room,
Claiming you as its kind, pours round your head in bloom,
So melting where it flows that the strong, armour-browed
Skull seems as pervious as a cloud;

Or seems a field of corn by the wind liquefied
Streaming over the arches of a round hill-side.
Contours and skin make tender the planes of light and shadow
The pale and darker gold of the upland meadow.

Only for a moment your cavernous human brow
Will dwell in the world of sense as naturally as now,
Beautiful with no meaning, but that it commands
Those to love, who hold you in their hands.

Child Waking

The child sleeps in the daytime,
With his abandoned, with his jetsam look,
On the bare mattress, across the cot's corner;
Covers and toys thrown out, a routine labour.

Relaxed in sleep and light,
Face upwards, never so clear a prey to eyes;
Like a walled town surprised out of the air –
All life called in, yet all laid bare

To the enemy above –
He has taken cover in daylight, gone to ground
In his own short length, his body strong in bleached
Blue cotton and his arms outstretched.

Now he opens eyes but not
To see at first; they reflect the light like snow,
And I wait in doubt if he sleeps or wakes, till I see
Slight pain of effort at the boundary

And hear how the trifling wound
Of bewilderment fetches a caverned cry
As he crosses out of sleep – at once to recover
His place and poise, and smile as I lift him over.

But I recall the blue-
White snowfield of his eyes empty of sight
High between dream and day, and think how there
The soul might rise visible as a flower.

Song for a Young Mother

There, there, you fit my lap
Like an acorn its cup,
Your weight upon my arm
Is like a golden plum,
Like an apple in the hand
Or a stone on the ground.

As a bird in the fallow
Scoops a shallow hollow
Where the earth's upward pressing
Answers egg and nestling
– Earth's mass the beginning
Of all their learning –

So you learn from my arm
You have substance and a home.
So I learn from your birth
That I am not vague and wild
But as solid as my child
And as constant as the earth.

All Children's Beauty

All children's beauty is dear
To me because of you
As yours is for all children's sake.

One crying in park or street,
From misery or beating will,
Plucks across space a note from a nerve tuned by you.

And when you cry, to whom I can run to bring peace,
I think of the unappeasable crying
Of children starved in Poland or in Greece.

Flowers of Almond

Begotten in our war's mid-winter, shoots of faith,
The children spangling early spring seem the cold flowers
Of almond on black twigs like pearls of gum pressed forth.
Children are always strewn on earth, but these are ours,

And we are weak in faith, and we can thwart conceiving.
What pressed these heavenly drops, these stars, from our dark
    branches?
Our own, or all mankind's importunate believing?
On the white sky, in the north wind, how bold their dances.

Children Among Us

The children who inhabit here
And change our furniture
And scatter in our air
Their pollen out of catkin hair
And whose lives thread
Between our feet, between our hands, along the branches of our
    head –

We build with thought and work and time
A solid house for them
And there they partly dwell,
Willow herb in a cleft of wall,
Or like sun's fires
That light at dusk in a west room briefly on red and orange
    flowers;

Or doves in a high loft they are
That must launch into air
Yet wheel like bells about,
And round each change with the deepest note,
Curve home, compose
Their wings: and so our children, coming or calling, toll their
    need of us.

The Midsummer Meadow

The child's hair falls in hay-pale ribbons.
Her fair face bird's-egg-freckled, brooded warm by sun,
As I lie in the meadow, is
Printed above me on the poplar trees,
Subdued clear flame; like flame, seen after gone.

Warm apparition, living ghost,
How well you fit and like one of its fountains rise
Out of the silver flux of the day,
Out of the watery, always far away
Light on the poplar leaves, out of the sky's

Intensity that seems darkness
Beyond the leaves; while from the grass its flowers of brome,
Of oat and cocksfoot, rising single
Each in its garden of clear space, dissolve and mingle
To under-water shadow run with light of foam.

A Face

Nothing more beautiful will come my way
Than his face tilted where it lay,
Lay as it happened in my elbow's crook
(A child of four), yet with that look
Of lit from farther than the stars. His eyes
Were shut, and other gates likewise
That give on the world, though his nape knew where best,
Rumpling my sleeve, to come to rest;
Then lay in living stillness. Nothing here
But lines by chance handsome, skin clear
As children's is; but meaning with such power
Flowed through, I could have watched an hour;
As on a bridge above a waterfall
We watch one form, through which flows all.

Children Asleep

They enter their appearances at night –
Dispersed in deeds and volatile all day.
Their bodies still as stone and closed mouths say
More than day's twittering songs and swallow-flight.

They fall asleep and the day's hours fall
Like cornflower wreaths back from their humid hair,
Their radiating brows upturned to air,
Their open hands, and from their loosed limbs all.

At evening they came home bearing their sheaves.
I see their lives' appurtenances round them.
Yet here they lie as though solitude had found them.
The robins here might cover them with leaves.

IV

Shadows of Chrysanthemums

Where the flowers lean to their shadows on the wall
The shadow flowers outshine them all,
Answering their wild lightness with a deeper tone
And clearer pattern than their own
(For they are like flames in sun, or saints in trance,
Almost invisible, dissolved in radiance).

But space in that shadow world lengthens, its creatures
Fall back and distance takes their features;
The shadows of the flowers that lean away
Are blurred like milky nebulae;
And faint as though a ghost had risen between
The lamplight and the wall, they seem divined, not seen.

The dying wild chrysanthemums, the white,
Yellow and pink are levelled in light;
But here in their shadows, tones remain, where deep
Is set on deep, and pallors keep
Their far-off stations, and the florets more
Subtly crisp their bright profiles, or are lost in the flower.

An Elegy

In early winter before the first snow
When the earth shows in garden beds
(For the foam is blown of flower-heads
And the gardener has cut low
Or tied in place the stock and green)
When the world wears an inward mien
Of mourning and of deprivation,
The appearance fits this time and nation.

In early winter before the first snow,
The child whose steps began in June
In the short misty afternoon
Walks in the mournful park below

81

Branches of trees, and standing stretches
Her arms and sings her wordless catches.
Like light her play and happiness
Flicker on the world's distress.

In this city still unraided
Where the queues stretch round the corners
It befits us to be mourners
Who read of other lands invaded,
Who have heard at night death pass
To northern cities over us.
It befits us who live on
To consider and to mourn.

The quiet days before the snow,
The child's feet on the yellowing grass –
How can I make a rite of these
To mourn the pang I do not know,
Death fastened on the life of man?
Sorrow uses what it can.
Take as my rite this winter tune:
The child's walk in the darkening afternoon.

Barbara

When will she meet her face? Surely it is her fate –
Surely to claim her, this year, next year, soon.
Famished in that tower-shell, one watches late
At unlit windows, white sunflower to the moon.
A ghost of beauty watches in her face –

She who is common English, downright, gay,
Clumsy in speech and movements; like a schoolgirl smitten,
Thrown down and chained and loving to obey
Her husband, the young soldier; loving her grey kitten.
(No children till the war is over.)

Not for the present – which is war
Without high danger, the dust of separation –
This face seems built; it is an empty, haunted tower.
But when she is moonish and absent in conversation
I wonder if she has entered there,

And if those sculptured bones and southern eyes can be
Chance heritage; or are her other self, deeper than dreams;
Or are her future or potentiality.
I hardly hope so; for a tragic legend seems
Half written there, or written, half erased.

In a Safe Area

Life is changed, death is nearer; more will die younger
And suddenly; though here,
Here in the university city
The sirens call like owls
In the expected faithful evening
(Yet the heart stops); though here
Chestnuts in gales of down thud on the pavements.
The bombs we say are louder, but not near.

How to deny beauty like easy weeping –
How to escape delight
In all appearances this gold October
While London's refugees
Bestrew our streets like leaves, beautiful in number
These too that drift and press.
How can I cast my half-imagination,
Impiety of happiness?

Autumn Gardens

The flowers of autumn, the yellow and mauve,
Feed like fire in a slow stove
On the year's hoarded sun. The flowers and the days
Are warm and fruit-like now.

                          I half, through haze
Of hands and hair of the child with me,
See cabbages, purple of weed under sea,
In the park allotments; and asters by soft weather
Plum-bloomed, by sun and mist dissolved together.

In suburban gardens the sunflower generations
Follow on, as stars through the night to their stations,
And wherever out of hand wild ragwort blazes
There is blue binding smoke of Michaelmas daisies.

The Fire in the Grate

The fire with hollow note
Like a cluck, purring, or a dove's
Calling in deep caves of throat
Or caverned water, moves

As confidently in its sphere
Self-occupied, as though its wanderings were bound,
Like a bee's or a child's on ground,
By its own nature and its little power.

The tired close their eyes and hear
How it makes a living peace and sucks away care
By its quick sentient creature's voice and way,
Like the child busy with his life in play,
Who gives breath also, fanning the heart's air.

The February Hedge

The ash-tree's saplings spring and pour
With falling water's power and curve
As if the sky called them, the sky their floor,
The sun's the gravity they serve.

Bow of water; scythe's arc
To part the air. – Oh see the metal-light
And smooth stem seeking the bud's lustreless dark,
There pouring out of sight.

In a Flat

On these lonely evenings, we
In our high flat like a child's house in a tree
Hear the cars run by, as far
Remote from us in their impersonal star
Yet as close as wind or rain –
Their sound with use grown natural,
　　Engines of car and plane.

And we before our fire, as still as in a spell,
In our two bodies, in our lives as parallel,
Reading, or I sewing, we are camped together
Like travellers in unknown country in wild weather.
In our eyes' love visions of snow and distance also brood,
And like a third, a hearth-mate dog between us,
　　Lies the crystal solitude.

A Window

Here infinite as air
The fabric of the poplars fills the window square –
Invisible from the room's hollow
Their roots between the gardens, and where they break on sky,
And the eye cannot follow
Their argument of branch and twig; but signs – appearings –
Gleam of these, summer-lightning-free
In the leaves' cloudy clearings.

For its sky, the window space
Is filled with these dissolving garden-distant trees;
Filled with their pulse and breathing more
Than form – that seem unformed and subtle as the sea's
Landscape out of sight of shore;
Filled with their living water's sound like seas or rain;
As if an altar to earth's flux rose here –
Our breath of life, our constant air.

Daylight Alert

When the daylight Alert has sounded, calling us
To what? not fear but application – we seem to have stepped
   across
A line in time, like a low wall that nettles guard,
Into a place marked off, an orchard or unkept graveyard.

The long gust sinks to peace, children who cried recover
Their joy; we stand in grass and look, the low wall is crossed over.
This is another realm where silence is so loud,
The sky shines so, the grass springs thicker, the fruits rush and
   thud.

Bombs have not fallen on our town; the shoppers scarcely
Lift eyes to the clear sky and fighters crossing straight and
   sparsely.
Our blood no more than smiles at this *memento mori*
As if it were a skull in flowers or a pale murder story.

Only our souls say in the stillness of their breath:
This is the hour that may be ours, the hour of pain and death.
What are we waiting for? What are we stretched to meet
Here in a walled and haunted plot set in our shopping street?

The hour shuts like a flower or dream when it is ended,
The far wall come upon too suddenly, the All Clear sounded.
It was not death but life we were called to entertain,
Waving to one who flashed so fast by in a royal train;

Called not to death but thought, still called to application,
Standing with empty eyes, dropped hands, at the small railway
    station,
On the flowered country platform, we who have come so far
To honour one we never meet – wind, is he? Falling star?

A Naturalist

The stones and dust seemed flowers in the lane's warm shade.
He in his dust-white coat went down through the breached
Low wall by the road into a flowering glade
Where the small briars his hand, the cow-parsnip reached
His shoulder, with flower-heads, level umbels spread
On their thick fluted pillars, head beyond head.

Spacing the parsnip flowers and passenger rose,
The grass like air stood everywhere in channels.
There he thigh-deep, a patient man in flannels,
With his glass-green net still, and in repose
His heavy thoughtful head, seemed rooted in the brome,
Stock of that natural garden, never so at home.

Leaves of Elm

This is the day set for the elms to cast
Their clear yellow leaves, not blown to earth but loosed
As though a hand opened and let them go,
Fall in still air and light unjarred like snow.

87

The elms with their country look that were hedge trees
Before the houses came, now with their knees
In buddleia and prunus, behind the low brick walls
Standing at relict intervals

Hold gathered under each, over garden path and street, a pool
Of leaves like a shadow or the pale burning, on a dull
Surface, of light reflected, when it seems to dwell
– Light so intense yet soft as gloom – within the answering wall.

The Tree on Christmas Eve

All things that beam like water and like snow
Faceted glance and sparkle cover
The little spruce tree. Frosty rivers flow
Along its branches, weighted over
As if by snow's lax watery load, by clasps
Of candles and hung moons of glass.

A stranger in the room, yet the room's heart
And its cold silver midnight hearth;
Candles unlit, yet streams of light flow out;
The tree one flower, like moonlit earth,
Flower without face, yet does tonight possess
The face's flower and crown of singleness.

Cut Tulips

They have come so far, the yellow tulips, in their streaming
Towards the sun that half dissolved in light they seem
(With their path lost, first certainty and single face)
To gaze with an unspeakable wild consciousness;
Throat laid to ground like stags, mouth lifted up to bell;
Still in their changed and yielded forms grace cannot fail.

An Overshadowed Holiday

That low-noted holiday
The bats signed with their flight
Sudden as touch, below the bridge, in the shallows of light,

When bodied from the river's beam
The swans homed, circling round
Near the bus station and the soldiers' gathering ground.

Even day was twilight: vague our words
And thoughts in public rooms,
And drift of leaves by the bar the service uniforms.

Even noon by the September river
Cast a light like shadow
On fruit of guelder rose in a protected meadow,

A light like sleep on the tall flowers,
Willow herb, loosestrife
And surf of umbels: sun that gave dispersed their life

To evening light, gemmed and dark-white –
That all day loitering there
We walked in sun, yet slept in the forest shade of the air.

A Vapour Trail over the Park

And the families go home
And the ducks stand on the weed,
And the leaves set broad to sun
Have taken all they can.

The baby as the beeches loom
Prints his full face and heavy lids
(By sunlight, like the day, washed pale)
On a dark green deep.

And time might sleep; but vertical
Dropping, slow, invisible,
A plane divides the sky's blue cliff
With a mountain waterfall.

Women Shopping with Young Children

Limpid along the pavement flowing in a dream
She is stopped on a stone, a human voice and hand.
Then what pain and confusion rock the rearing stream!
I wait between the dark-dressed column of our friend
And her, spread on the railings in a fan of foam,
Till the world sways to rest, the drops have fallen home,

And she, as if just wakened, sees the equable neighbour,
A basket of cartons and fruit, the baby boy in the pram,
And sets herself to amuse the boy with wild behaviour,
Streaming away and back, drawing his eyes from him;
And our eyes move like hands after her as we talk
Of shops and news of war, and when the boy will walk.

A Refugee

My heart had learnt the habit of earthly life
In an accustomed place.
My voice had learnt the habit of maternal
Sharpness and gentleness.

My thighs had learnt the speech of love. The house
And market tasks that show
So small a flower, rooting in hands and feet
Had matted my flesh through.

My husband died in the mercy of Russian snow.
My child died in the train,
In three days in the weeping cattle truck
From Breslau to Berlin.

I was not taught the song of extremity,
The dancing of duress.
All that I know of infinite is the intensity
Of finite tenderness.

All that I have of goodness is through love –
Their love my only worth.
My rigid arms set in the shape of their love
Have no more use on earth.

A Dark World

Under the pent-house branches the eight swans have come,
Into the black-green water round the roots of the yew;
Like a beam descending the lake, the stairway to their room.

The young swans in their tender smoke-grey feathers, blown
By wind or light to a faint copper smouldering,
Come docile with their parents still, three-quarters grown.

The old swans, built of light like marble, tower and scatter
Light in the dusk; but the young are mate to the yew's shade.
With their dim-green webbed feet like hands they part the water

And wind among its loops and eyes of mercury
Less visible than these they have wakened; and beside
The trellised roots they twine their necks as fine and grey.

In groups and in their fugue following one another
They turn to constant music their intercourse; and passing
With neck stretched on, with greyhound brow, brother by brother,

Or slowlier drawing level, where their mute and furled
Wings touch they loose a feather to float on the night-face
Of water, with white stars to drift as a dark world.

View from a Bus Stop

There is a mist on the dark thoroughfare,
The long road leading north out of the town,
Like bloom on sloe or plum. Either the air
Still winks with night haze or it is the down
Of buds from trees reflected that unfocuses
The roofs above the grass and dove-grey crocuses.

The near is crossed with distance. The road seems
A fair width like the Thames at Westminster.
Under the lorries the road surface dreams,
Brimming like water. A red bus from far
Halts at a crossing up the road from ours
On the other side, grazing the almond flowers.

A Summer Day

In the transparent silk of the air
Enhanced as if by distance and yet near;
Lustred as distance yet across
The narrow field and reeds of the river close,
The elder trees are cast against the base
Of ash woods hung on the cliff of limestone's face;

And on their lithe twigs looped in bowers
They lift the faint green of their curded flowers.
The stream flows near with all along
White and veiled mauve the heads of comfrey hung,
And mauve the small and dusty flowers of nettle
Where dragonflies like their own shadows settle

Rarely, on restless wings of black,
Latticed, and here opaque. Their glinting back
Flashes with blue-green depth like seas;
And this late summer, this first of summer days
These princes of sun emerged move in such herds
As fish or common flies or flocking birds.

The Half-Mown Meadow

I walked in a half-mown flowering meadow by the sea's-
Edge of the grass, where yesterday the mower went.
Bloomy and purple as clover were the fog-grass and bent;
The field so wide, it broke on misty boundaries.

The stubble and mown hay were fresh like tidal sand
When at low tide I walked by that standing lake-waved sea;
The surface of the grass wore such fluidity,
Melting of plane in plane, as seemed unknown on land.

Our eyes rest on the sea like gulls and find a home
In that infinity. My eyes would not be called
By the small flags of ash-trees in the hedge, or belled
Flocking of children, from the sea where they had come,

Whose sky-reflecting waves, mantled with darkness under,
In waves' compulsive ways bred form on form of light;
Whose currents far from land carried fordone my sight;
All colour at the full as in a time of thunder.

The Day of Widowhood

This is the shadow of her weddingtide,
And she again distinguished like a bride.
The shadow falls certain from that day's sun
Since what is done in time must be undone.

Caught in a shaft of darkness, strange her grey
Dim well-deep face lies on the coloured day,
On wind and flowering grass and rain held high,
With trees like rain slanted against the sky.

But her eyes inward turned watch by the bed and tomb
Of her long marriage; by his face in death become
All profile like a mountain range. O height of face,
O earth stamped with unyielding singleness!

Herself again pierced on a height and crowned,
She looks across the lower soft and broken ground
To the first peak of love; and to her view
Her life is simple, hung between these two.

Who bore and nursed his children here at length
Has borne him over death, death giving strength;
And vision dwells in her extremity,
Peace in her thought: "This is what was to be."

Though her mouth's weeping tremulous denies
Vision and peace, and though his absence cries
Like a night bird, and though the common seeks to cover,
What is done in eternity will not be grassed over.

After Midsummer

Love, we curve downwards, we are set to night
After our midsummer of longest light,
After hay harvest, though the days are warmer
And fruit is rounding on the lap of summer.

Still as in youth in this time of our fruition
Thought sifts to space through the words of definition,
But strangeness darkens now to a constant mood
Like hands shone dark with use or hafts of wood;

And over our dense days of activity
Brooding like stillness and satiety
The wonder deepens as clouds mass over corn
That here we are wakened and to this world born

That with its few colours so steeps and dyes
Our hearts, and with its runic signs implies
Meaning we doubt we read, yet love and fear
The forms more for the darkened light they bear.

It was so in youth too; now youth's spaces gone
And death of parents and our time's dark tone
Shadow our days – even children too, whose birth
And care through by-ways bring our thoughts to death;

Whose force of life speaks of the distant future,
Their helplessness of helpless animal nature;
Who, like the old in their shroud of age, close bound
In childhood, impress our natural pattern and end.

The springy twigs arch over walls and beds
Of lilac buddleia, and the long flower-heads
Run down the air like valleys. Not by force
But weight, the flowers of summer bend our course;

And whether we live or die, from this time on
We must know death better; though here as we stand upon
The rounded summit we think how softly the slope
And the sky have changed, and the further dales come up.

Above the Bay

The wind can like a rodent wield
Body and tail one lash coiling faster than light
On the late uncut corn fluted and carved to sight,
On the thin flaxen barley in the outmost field.

Below the cliff the fan-shaped tide,
Flowing in power to fill the bay, lies to the height
A fan of figured ivory hollow and white.
At such a dream-bound pace the crescent breakers glide,

Their form seems from their force distilled
Awhile; above the rocks the spray held long unbreaking
Falls without salt or shock; the waves' fixed overtaking
Is stillness, and their pouring snows are glacier-stilled.

Over the leaden valleys, high
Hung between range and range, their whiteness dies dispersed
Like sea-bird's wreck; while new the surf buds from the crest
Pausing, withdrawn, and flowers in ruin finally.

The apron-waves, the flats of foam
Stay at the wet sand's rim – a pause so long and full
One might dream ankle-deep there like cattle in a pool
An hour before the down-wash draws and the fresh surges come.

A Web of Mist

A web of mist is over sea and land.
Black slugs are grazing on the diamonded grass.
The sea slants like a banner lying on the wind
Or like a photograph of the moon's face,

Smooth out of mist; yet in its weaving show
Faint horizontal flaws, and the transparency
Is brushed and finger-printed with the wind's shadow
Blurring the rocks' maroon clear under sea.

The cliffs seem forested almost to base,
So furred with green of bracken, honeysuckle, heath.
The drifts of rain are thoughts crossing a sightless face.
The gulls glide up the steep sea underneath.

Inland the tall grass bows its grain, the lower
Lace-headed bents are nets of dew. The avenues
Of meadowsweet and every cloud-white umbel flower,
Though winding, close in mist before their close;

A Wood-Pigeon in October

Beyond the level windows of the second floor,
Past the transparent tissue of the sycamore
Yellowed in clammy autumn air,
The wood-pigeon that built a nest in the pine tree
Brooding above the street without anxiety
Has hatched her pair.

In her economy she blankets them in feathers
Fluffing her body to an O against all weathers,
Rounding grey back and Michaelmas breast,
And feeds them from her crop, and takes the time to sit
Like a fruit of the bough, moved in the wind with it,
She and her nest.

Or as a street-lamp, or at dusk the indoor light
Or fire reflected in the window hangs on night
And seems to burn in leaves, so she
Nursing the natural hearth, the brazier of her heart
To warm her self and young, all night shines in our thought,
Though dark of dark to see.

In an Autumn of Fear

These autumn gardens have a look of depth like air,
So that our eyes find space and breathing there.
These autumn flowers with their mountain colourings
Grow higher, wilder, in stranger ways than spring's,
Answering with bounty those who ask for proof,
As if they said *Infinity is enough*,
Said *Innocence is endless, life a perpetual*
Fountain. And we who dream our age's fall,
Each alone pacing his cell of common fear,
Find hope in the wildness of the fall of the year.

Relict

Now the old man upstairs in the westward-looking room,
In the extending chair with a rug on his knees,
Who put by rug and book and lifted in welcome
His height that seemed too high for safety – he and these,
His books and chair, now they are gone, on the small house
Set in the amber street the walls do not fall in,
Though the rooms narrow down, lost their calling and use,
The life that flows in them diminished, feminine.

She who, past change, must change, stricken too late for cure,
The wife has far become mere loss and waiting age.
Yet still the living, who turn to the living, turn to her
And time with bramble hooks more plucks at her passage,
With ancient loves, new pains, importunes to death's gate,
With body's needs and fine anxieties sharp as briars,
And binds in dollshouse state and order, and bids wait
In the autumn suburb, in its painted world's-end fires.

There where to visit her is to speak and commune
With one of autumn's leaves – though fireless pewter laid
On their gold, strange as a spoken word in a bright tune,
Yet one of them, of their exhausted substance made,
And seeming as they do, tethered in space, use gone,
Indrawn, directionless, more wholly to appear
And more to exist, being for being's sake alone,
And saying as they say: "All that I am is here."

Her present hour's insistence, her routines and cares
Dazzle this deep ground tone of her facing towards dark –
But not conceal. We cannot tell how the night airs
Washing against her house walls lift and float that ark
From the safe street into what seas. She lights our state –
Between the lightning's branches, her faint constant beam –
Saying, we too, through all our days we are still and wait.
This is the breath of life in our life's real dream.

The Clover Fields

The fields are overcast with light at evening,
With marguerites increased, a chalk-white settling,
With mist of the damp breath of clover leaves and grasses
And slanting light reflected from their press of faces.

And close the earth shows parchment through, though netted
    over
With the fresh-dark entangled green and shade of clover,
The leaves ornate, the perfect narrow trefoils set
Thick as in tapestry, and little flowering yet.

And time stands like a soul; the summer's hardly flowing
Twilight stands in the fields that look towards their mowing,
Still as a man might stand in his own fields contemplating.
The meadows give their answer to this hour of waiting.

Sketches of Elder Trees

I

Across the narrow arm of the lake, the wild weed elder
Spreading over the grass-land comes, a flock to water,
Caught in the painted day descending
The stairway slope, the leaders bending
Branches to drink. It is their grouping, pressed and herded,
That prints the trees with motion held, with undivided
Outlooking animal awareness –
Their grouped descent, through the day's clearness.

II

Elders that grow in angles of a wall and lean
Their arched and offering branches from a base of stone,
And those that build like birds in hedges thicket-grown,
Themselves their citadel, their five-foot wall of green –
First shrub to leaf in spring its light wild skeleton –

Now all are summer-bound, self-sheltered, tented down.
And now in June's high fold, at the year's pause they spread
And lift like a stemmed plate of sweets their flowering head,
And green as light on white through leaves or water shed
Their moonrise green of bud before their flowers are blown.

Evening Scene

The waves lay down their trail,
On the brown water feathers of foam.
Over the dark bituminous sands
The stragglers loiter home.

Where the stream seeps to sea
And the sands are a tarnished glass to the sky
They walk as if on evening light,
They run and seem to fly.

The shallow acre-wide
Waves of low tide swathe their feet like a meadow.
Surely they feel themselves unmade,
Spirits that cast no shadow.

I see them small, distinct,
Dark, and see on the sheen of what wings they fly,
The two lit wings of land and sea,
The one vane of the sky;

And see, not near nor far,
The black-brown cliffs stand with their slopes of green
Stippled with darkness. All of space
Is the sand's width between.

Return from the Beach

Across the sands burdened with their dark tone,
With heat of honey and with seams of stone-
Blue shade under the day-long azure,
The holiday-makers turn from pleasure,

Turn from the brilliant west in twos and fours,
In groups dispersed and quiet, with their powers
Of play before the light failing,
With trailing child and his spade trailing;

The women bearing their weight, the youths their lightness,
The outriding boys still in a mould of brightness,
The girl tranced by beatitude,
The man pleased with his hardihood,

All in their human posture pacing on
As if they carried their lives in the form of a crown.
Late cricketers, a lingering couple
With gulls possess the world of opal.

A Wood of Lilac

I only once saw a wood of lilac – more than three
Or four together, light by darker purple massed
In gardens. That wild grove had every stem a tree,
A thicket of white lilac with its loose and tossed
Habit and flowers like surf or flakes of light on sea.

This time of year, the garden lilacs light by dark,
The curtained morning bird-songs inexhaustible
Over the rich gardens, the cuckoo most of all
Emptying the sky of these from heavens beyond the park
Bring to my mind that wood of white lilac run wild.
The birds seem foam-born there, the cuckoo even might build.

Michaelmas Summer

Each day we waken to a summer day,
Till the whole summer seems a summer day
That opens on an estuary of evening
Endless, as any summer morning may,

When light seems not to change unless to increase
By the slow settling of its ash of peace.
So in this Michaelmas summer whose days
Are evening hours, which are eternities,

Each day lays down – like bees that one by one
File into time – its apple, aster, sun;
Each day lays down a coal on the slow fire
Of the real season and this miraged one

That seems it cannot end; each day of summer given
Beyond longing, feeds in us the illusion or the vision
Of Heaven on Earth, of Heaven in Heaven.

Autumn Borders

The flowers of autumn borders set before brick or stone,
Flowers of the year's decline after the equinox
Are the highest and wildest, as though they strained towards
    sun,
Though the sun enters like a bee with level flight,
Though the young gardener strips to the waist in warmth and light
To weed as if he bathed in the blue daisy-shocks.

There bees hang like a steam drawn from the flowers, and printed
With flame, brighter than leaves, the butterflies return
From narrow circuits, tortoiseshell and the indented
Comma, return to their same field of flower faces,
To a known foothold on a ground of purple daisies,
Or spread on dim pink orpine their vermilion.

Between the mounds and thickets the slight anemones loosen
And space at intervals of stars their porcelain-white
Flowers and those pink-tinged like strains of bramble blossom –
Seven-branched, on rushing stems. The burning dahlias fade,
Heavy and solitary, to an ochreous shade.
From one day to the next the year turns to its night.

November Afternoon

The light is a feeble flood over the meadow
But the river under its low bank is in shadow.

The oarsmen wait for the lock to clear
On the tranced water hanging over the weir.

In their white singlets they droop arm and shoulder
And know the passing of time as the air falls colder.

The few pale heart-shaped poplar leaves are bright
Beyond, selected by the searching light.

In November

By rivers and in gardens in this brown November
Between the nameless bird-brown tones of fawn and umber
In fading leaf and fallow stem and open tree
We walk on Earth's transparency,

Through scenes that all as one like curtains sway, that faintly
Doubtfully breathe and sigh like a sleeper watched intently;
Where low skies stretch to infinite the river shores
And formal gardens' corridors

And children play on the sodden grass. The elm-trees' rare
Yellow leaves are subdued as light on their mouse-hair.
They race in childhood's legendary pastures; we
In our habit of maturity

Walk on transparent Earth in autumn sieved with space,
On Earth of light withdrawn and flowering called to base,
And tissue of atoms torn – yet most now, all in jeopardy,
Teacher to us of truth, form of reality.

The Death-Bed

"I died in bed, in age, at home, alone,
Although among my own yet with none known,
In kindness of strangers, strangeness of my kin
Whose votive eyes were turned to death's not mine,
My death so changing them they died for me
To nameless shades of mere humanity.

"Thinner than air, they had no power to keep
My recognition summoned by the deep
Engaging themes of young maturity,
When between forward dream and reverie
Of age, between all guessed-at and all done,
My love and path were found and children born.

"There memory lapsed and roaming, once I said
(Propped in a foreign land on a strange bed)
'This is my wedding day', and saw on their pale
Devoted lips the image of my smile,
Bashful and winning; for no other mirror
They held to me to teach me truth or terror.

"A shade they called my daughter came to me.
I stirred and spoke of my young family
That I must care for: when I would have risen
I felt my weakness and the bed my prison,
Yet thought I should not die, so strangely I seemed then
To have known a later time, awake or dreaming.

"But the dream worn to fragmentary sand
Sounded in sleep; what more I understand
Untellable."
                              The watchers say
"It seemed we died your death, yourself so far away,
Free in your past, in sleep; and yet it was not so.
Forgive us our life and that we let you go."

Roman Hyacinths and Christmas Tree

The Christmas flowers are shaped like conifers,
Of the dark tree the white obverse.
The tree is a night sky that underlies
And silvers its embroideries,
And only through its darkness shine, so far
Spaced on its midnight branches, moon and star.
There the light touches down in flight and takes
The sheen of webs and falls and flakes.

The silver hyacinth, though in its flower
It follows the tree's spread and spire,
Out of its time an essence has arisen
Of light, adorned by the dark season;
Wearing the shadowed air between its curled
Petals as human beauties wear the world;
Wearing our age of nightfall and black frost
Like sable ribbons at its breast.

Your flowers as fresh as green, with green shadow
Touched, and your leaves as bright as snow,
And all your breathing airs, fine to an arrow
Whose path of light is hard to follow.
Flower of clear bells, plain in complexity,
It is earth's darkness lights your light for me.
Innocence lost, the long way must become
For men and worlds the shortest path to home.

Fragility of Happiness

In summer, in a kind environment,
Green city or suburb or country picnic place,
Our children playing with their peers content
Their parents' eyes with their happiness and grace.

Like the movement of the leaves of fire or trees
By which we dream, like the movement of the shallows
Of air and time we breathe by, now by these
Moving, we love, the tide flows in our hollows.

Oh yet, in these painted hours that come and go,
How the mild surface scene hums with its deep!
We ride a sea of space and darkness, though
White on its glass the swans of the sky now sleep.

V

February Landscape

The pools of smooth-skinned water circle
Down the swollen river.
Beyond the branch where the grey-painted
Foot-bridge crosses over,
Grey of the sky, the high-hung gate swings.
The cattle are taken in.
Near and beyond, the drab and heavy
Waters shine and shine.

Still locked, the twigs of thorn and willow
Glisten. The dusty elder
Strange in small leaf sits in the wintry
Landscape spring bewilders.
Loose-reined between the river and further
Floods two riders pass,
And swans stand where like snow late-lying
Are flood-pools pricked with grass.

Garden Sonnets

I SINGLE PEONY

Chestnut and holm-oak and the tulip tree
Are shadowers of college lawns, between
Whose walls of stone deeper the drifts of green
Form than in open fields; whose peony
Is redder than wild poppies. Now the dense
And globe-round bud risen compact and close
Breaks to a flowing grace, as hands fall loose.
Yet the red of the flower is a well of reticence.

Flower out of China, though long domiciled
Like the garden trees, keeping as alien mark
Tincture's intensity well-deep and dark:
How it draws eyes with that, where on its field
Of strong and copious mid-green leaves the cup
Lies wide, with yellow stamens lifted up.

The lights are moonlight on the copper beech,
But for a scattering fall of sun direct
Over one shoulder, single leaves reflect.
This far side where no strays of sun can reach
The leaves are carved by moonlight each from each.
Through dusk of spring their undeciphered colour
Under its shadowing bloom has ripened fuller;
Now night builds like a dove in cleft and breach.

The flowering chestnuts are sunlit and rounded.
I study this dark, delta-branching tree,
Stream flowing to its moonlit estuary
Out of the mountain rocks where it is grounded.
I touch the leaves clammy with honeydew
And trace the veins that the dark blood runs through.

Peony

The flowers rest light in leaves touched with red like them,
And the dye at the base of the petals runs in the stem.
Light fills the great pale ornamental flower
As the skies between its petals are filled with air.
Light and lightness, penetrability,
Have laid on its slow growth against gravity
A look of doves in their slow rising, air under wings,
And a look on its paleness laid, of cloud openings.

Her Coughing Wakened Me

Her coughing wakened me in a strange bed
At a strange daylight hour empty and bright,
And to her strange, familiar company
Whose room I had moved into over-night.

110

Frost on the flowers and grass this first of May;
And clogged with dreams I made the gas-fire burn
To warm the air she breathed. I had been childless
And loveless in my ravening sleep alone.

Confused with bird-song bells rang from a tower
And seemed hallucination. I brought water,
Linctus to soothe her throat and smoothed her hair,
The dignified, pale child changed for my daughter.

There passed an hour eternal while the bells
Rang for May Morning, while her cough would dredge
My soul from sleep, and intermittent words
As light as bird-flocks scattering in a hedge

Brushed me with wings. Strange our communication
In the hollow of the morning. On her features
Was the patience of all sick children, and a general
Sweetness lay over her own, her single nature's.

An Old Woman Reflects

My life was a novel read by the fire on a winter
Evening between supper and sleep.
My manner of reading is greedy, blind and deep.
The latch was down, no one could enter.

The story was long, and the elders mid-way died;
The child turned woman, the heat-haze lifted;
And stilly at times, the contours sank or shifted
As when deep tunnellings subside.

And the interest spread through branches, generations –
The tale grown complex, wide and shallow.
Yet most towards the end came (if I follow)
Echoing themes, returning passions.

Little it all may mean; little and all.
For I plunged in it as one may in dreams;
I gave myself, four hours by the clock it seems,
To its truth of dream, to its dream-clear call.

111

O dreamed, confused, headlong and lingering
Life! Yet all things that came to me
Came, great and small, with such authority
As doves with tokens from a king.

Now I raise my eyes dazzled. The forms, the bright
Voices shred by, die echoing down.
I must return to life. Oh, I must turn
And lift the blind, and read the night.

By a River Bridge

If water were its sheen alone – but here
A child was drowned last year
By the bronze willows, no-one to erase
The panic from his face,
Nothing to answer his not comprehending,
Nothing but its ending.

Strange efflorescence of our world, or more
A spirit than a flower,
Visible beauty; silent apparition
Yet of such urgent mission:
Say in what language you are reconciled,
The bloom, with the drowned child.

Light and Flowers

Perfect, opaque – there seemed no way
In, no word for words to say.
Like the white moon clear in the sky by day

The white flowers hung on the blue wall
Distant in beauty, and the fall
Was absolute, no foothold there at all.

But set in the west window soon
As evening crumbles afternoon
And blue and white are merged and overthrown,

Those flowers that seemed only a little
Translucent, less than finest brittle
China, now stream with light through every petal.

Light wakes in them their own shadows,
Bringing them darkness, as it does
All textures it penetrates, water and glass;

And drowns, and lays on its flood-plain –
Filled with the breath of life again –
These that seemed once flowers of porcelain.

City Pigeons

Heavy the opal rose-green tame
Pigeons, that seem for all their flame's
Encumbered flickering, as bound
Stem-linked as flowers to the green ground,

Or sessile in the city's mown
Precincts as grave or building stone.
Heavy they rise when feet fall near them
And strange it seems that space will bear them,

And strange that flight is their condition
Like men who own pride and ambition –
These kin to lilac flower falls
And stones that form the roots of walls.

A Blue Day

On the clouded flaxen beaches
And on the moonstone-coloured stretches
Where the tide ebbs or streams are spread
Fanning to sea, the sky has laid
A wing of blue – on all that lies,
Water or land, between these eyes
And the indiscernible vanishing,
Has laid the one butterfly wing.

Ribbon streams of lighter blue,
Veining of leaf or wing, lead through
To a mirage of lagoons and coast
In the sulphur-touched, the scabious mist.
Here sheaves of ragwort rust to brown
From gold on stalk where the cliff runs down.
All else, the papery grass blades even
Are stained with blue by the gaze of heaven.

Day condensed to a butterfly's wing,
Earth to my eyes' range, following
From low cliff slopes – a little tower –
A sky-line undefined, not far:
Here in this circle arbitrary
I stalk my prize, reality,
Where the sky starts in the scene beneath
The soul contained, the bloom of breath.

At Sunset

Sky of sky, cerulean sky
Lightening towards green at evening, limpid glazed;
The pure tone of infinity
Under the arched updrawn, under the raised

Distraught brows of the violet cloud,
And in the upper fire the wreathed and curled
Tresses or feathers of a god
Not made like man or creature of this world.

Something flew up before we came,
As the sun set, out of the purple flowing
Round sea, some god or bird without a name.
This glamour is the wake and litter of its going.

Summer Night

The summer night is sea-blue still
Behind the street-lamps to the west and north
And downy seeds of poplar drift
Like gossamer on ankles and on mouth.

In midnight rooms the lagging day
On sheets and blankets leaves flood-pools of white,
That wait like summer sleeplessness
For new day's flow, beyond this feint of night.

A flower is pressed on the window pane:
White poppy, by translucence shadowed blue.
The children sigh in sleep, the hair
At the nape of their neck damp as with honey-dew.

Noon in the Botanic Garden

Feathered like leaves of the acacia
The world puts out its summer air
That lies, a lustre and a down,
On the stone trees of the academic town.

Heavy on the garden is the peace of summer.
The lilies straggle and fade sooner
In the light that everywhere
Lifts like a bindweed its white trumpet flower.

Few birds at midday, chaffinches and sparrows,
Drop down from trees to grass.
A white butterfly, one,
On steps of air climbs the high wall of stone.

115

And like a bee of this scholastic garden
– The heat her star – an iron-haired woman
Passes between the stems
From flower to flower, stooping to list their names.

A Woman at a Window

Under the window a brick-walled garden
By a suburban lane:
A nest it seemed, high-built or hollowed,
Set distant, on a different plane
From the gravelled way that passers followed.

So on the stage two scenes are given
Side by side; in either
A group performs, miming or speaking
As if unconscious of the other,
Though we see both, gods over-looking.

This Sunday I watch no drama, only
The ageless, quiet, dark,
Drawn on to church; couples together
With pigeon-pair set for the park
Through blossom and uncertain weather.

And the eye with its shallow passion
Sees all as innocent,
All as weather and flowering nature;
And those within the gate are lent
This bloom, with every other creature.

Yet all enhanced here, concentrated,
Even earth shows browner, bare
Between narcissi quick and dying.
The girl who curtains with her hair
Page and grass where she is lying,

The boy at gardening with his father,
Engrossed – I hear their words;
And not far different I suppose them
From others of earth's creatures, birds,
Trees, men, but to the heart that knows them;

But to the heart that makes its mastering
Distinctions, its enclaves
Here of eternity; from which beginning
Imagination, from the haunts it loves
Might break to colonize the world with meaning.

The Nest

Where the bird flew from under, lift the grass
– And strange to the open day, and strange to us,
The pipit's eggs as brown as water there
Answer the children's stare,
Darkly reflecting like pools in leafy places
Oval and dappled their unwritten faces.

Startled beneath its tussock, world or room
The small round cup concave like the sky's dome
Lies clear as still, and with under-water gleaming
Draws and constrains to dreaming.
The speckled eggs are crystal globes to gaze in
And see the spring and freshness of creation.

The children scatter who awhile have been
Caught in this glass, as pleased with all the scene,
With blue and yellow flowers and watered corn
And stream thatched dark with thorn;
And half forget; yet long their faces hold
Reflected beams shone from that new-found world.

One Wave

At the late end of evening when
Only the white remain
Printed on darkness, of all flowers
– White lilies and campanulas,
The white maroon-spotted foxglove –
And sweet and chilling damp airs move,

There is one moment when the white
Flowers are changed to gulls on night.
For night in waves flows like a sea,
Not imperceptibly.
There is one wave rocks the beached boat,
Lifts, and it is afloat.

A Short Night

She is in the garden weeding almost in darkness.
Indoors we say it is quite dark. Fetch her in.
Soon now the hedges will be filled with mist
At daybreak, in the bird's hour. Get her to come.
Call your wife, our hostess, home.

So she comes in, tranquil, grubby and vague
With gardening, bringing the scent of stock through the door,
Bringing her unbelief in time, with the frailty
Of the phantasmal summer night,
And makes us tea and puts the tray on the floor,
And the talk flourishes more than before.

After the Bright Day

After the bright day the land will secrete
Its darkness; the fawn sands will spin
Film on film from themselves of violet,
On which the nacreous deltas shine

Not brighter than the sky-clearings they image,
But wider and more constantly,
Under the faults in the cloud, the clefts, the mirage/
Of day laid white, low over sea –

After the sun; after stray clouds and wind
Have stroked, like hands against the pile,
To smokier the fur-bloom-coloured sand –
Blowing in desultory file

All day off sea; after the seagull's shadow
That driven as moth haunts the cliff-wall
Has crossed again, and the day-flowering rainbow
Has lived and died in the waterfall.

The Tall Hyacinth

Tomorrow stake and tie the plant;
For like a leaning tower,
Leaning with all its bells, the sky-pink flower
Bears on the air; the stem curves to recover
And the strong leaf-blades slant
Too high and wildly outwards or bow over.

Beautiful, grown so tall and rare;
Though a little overgrown,
A little winged and flighty for the brown
Bulb fibre in a window of the house
In a bowl of earthenware;
Almost for earth itself too tenuous.

But beautiful, so set for flight,
So straining at its tether,
And coloured like a pale flamingo feather
Or sunset light on cloud or mountain snow
Or any ground of white;
Most beautiful, expressive, soaring so.

The Garden Lake

)rifted with leaves to the dense, sheltering quarter,
˜he endmost harbour of the lake,
˜he swans in grey and chestnut-headed drake
˜arve their paths on the tessellated water.

The swan with breast-bone shaped like bows of ships,
Like ice-breakers that drive through floes
Divides the locking plane-leaves where it goes,
The heart-shaped poplar-leaves and willow-slips,

That give before it, melting with no pause
Like time or air most lightly pressed,
And settle after it, subside to their rest
Over the well-black pool of the wake it draws.

Now sieved through mist and branches, flecked and barred,
Gold and weak as the leaves, the sun
Raises a distant light on the grey of the swan
Like fire surmised, reflected on a cloud,

And paints the bronze-head drake sailing the fringes
Where the five-cornered plane-leaves lie
Like stars on outskirts of a galaxy;
And seems to pause here at the end of its ranges.

Two Notes on Parenthood

I THE WALL

I did not know I was to be
Built into a wall and weathered like a stone
To an anonymous ripeness of tone,
And with valerian and toadflax grown,
And all the future rest on me.

Then grow as plants do, merely grow.
Lightly enough we cannot touch you.
Though in a dream we seem to watch you
Skied on some stage, and we below
Divided by the impalpable lights,
Yet dreams arise only to pass,
And you must live entwined with us
Through years of actual days and nights.
Then be light-footed on the thin
Ice bridge above our deep crevasses.
Find pasture in our wildernesses.
All that we know, have done and been
Distils to a strange milk, and yet
You bless the bowl, drinking from it.

Growing Girl

Watching from the high brick wall
The younger children's tennis in the lane
Her eyes run thoughtless with the ball,
And the coasts of her face rise clear and plain.

Undiscovered or forsaken wholly
Against the sky those slopes and dunes lie now,
Moulded in natural melancholy
Of untilled country, chin and cheek and brow.

The hour absorbs the players and the girl
Dreaming above the clematis. The ball
Coming and going weaves its spell,

And her eyes with the ball run to and fro.
Only the tracts of cheek and temple know
She has a long journey to go.

The Outskirts of the Woods

They still come in the woods, netted in earth
And bramble, and each side the rutted path
In grass and papery leaves: wild strawberry
With infant flowers of white embroidery,
Like cities of pagodas blue of night
The bugle drifts, and on the limestone height
The emblematic rock-rose flat to light.

Taller and further, deer that love the shadow,
Bluebells herd; and where wood breaks down to meadow
And some rest in the shade of oaks and some
On the blue open brow, small vetches come,
Low among grasses hiding crisp and fine
Their leaflets, not their single blood-drop shine.
Small moths and flies have as delicate a line.

Here the gorse burns and here or anywhere
The barren honeysuckle may appear
Trailing its glaucous meditative leaves;
And in from here run those deep crypts and caves
That shelve and shelve to green obscurity
Where feet of roe-deer that we never see
Have bruised the seldom-glinting mercury.

A Kitten's Life

My friend's child had a kitten
Someone had weaned too young. I never heard
How it was brought into the child's possession.

A breath, a condensation
Of underlying vapour to faint cloud,
It seemed less animal than visitation;

Less like a cat than silver-
Smooth deep-sea fish brought strange and dumb to hand;
Fuller of distance than a journeying elver.

And yet its hardly-seeing
Sweet-slanting eyes (as now we understand)
In each direction looked towards not being.

Though it made no demands
They had given it what they could. It lay in wool
A week, touched milk, purred faintly in their hands.

On Mount Olympus wild
Our garden pansies grow, whose eyes recall
– *Viola gracilis* – kitten and child.

An Open-Air Performance of "As You Like It"

Art is unmade
To nature and the wild again
On the scythed grass before
A lime and skeletal ash
And the wall, solid with flowering,
Of longer unmown grass
Fumy with parsley flowers,
A level light mist rising;
Where the young actors barefoot,
Warm in their exaltation
Burn in the evening's chill.

The art the poet won
From wilderness dissolves again,
Unformed upon this formless stage
Confluent with all earth's air;
For infiltrating winds,
Laughter, mid-distant trains
Steal the speech from their voices,
Being amateur, unsure,
And moths bemuse their faces,
And our attention loses
Stragglers to cloud and star.

Envoys of life
At their set hour the swifts fly over,
Possess the air above us
And fish-tailed, fast as sight,
Play in their foamy margins,
Their intertidal light;
While the flood lamps yet hardly
Sophisticate earth's colours,
And we half ride with the birds
Over our audience faces,
Over the reckless words.

And when "If you have been..."
Orlando cries, "If ever been
Where bells have knolled to church..."
And sweet upon his words
The Christ Church evening bell
Answers the homesick youth
Like rhyme confirming verse,
Evidence crowning truth,
It seems to our delight
As though the poet's earth
And ours lay in one night;

As though we had heard
The bell before the words were made
With him. Therefore I love
All loose ends, distractions
At such performances,
All their imperfections;
And if we bring our children,
Their soft and stubborn questions
Threading the marble words;
And art delivered up
To nature and the wild again.

"King Richard II" at Stratford-on-Avon

1

Out of a sweetness nothing could increase –
So it must change or fall to less –
The evening landscape, wax to light
Like honey-comb and filled with it;
The ochre stain on dark trees here and there,
The one branch seized with fire,
And autumn daisies amethyst
Common as bonfire smoke or mist;

Out of our slow drive and our halting late
To watch across a pasture gate
The cattle branching from a ground
Of cloud and trees white-flooded round;
Out of our prelude and anticipation
That was itself fruition
We came with night to the white river swans
And white-invested Richard's tones.

2

Wound in his white cloud of imagination
Richard is dead, who had the mind to see
And saw his name a light in history,
Who read the cryptic words of his vocation
And answered dazzled and unluckily,
Wound in the white shroud of his fantasy.

Weakest of all, mere water, changed through watery
Prismatic opal to the shine of snow;
Against the rocks and seething, a bright bow
Blown with sea spray; weaker than flattery,
Subject to words and swords; through dream and show
And iron force falling to lie like snow.

Poet and actor raised this apparition,
A rainbow truth altering for every eye –
Not him who died in real obscurity
Slipping his life of ruin and negation
And left for Shakespeare's finding that *trouvaille*,
As if he had seen his name a light in poetry.

He died in real obscurity.
But our King Richard dies
Comforted by poetry
And tears of watching eyes
From century to century.

Here fused is all complexity:
His life; the imputed words;
And that male stride through history
Of heroes with their swords
The actors flash us from the boards.

Real and imagined mingle here
As colours fuse to white,
Or as the rays from everywhere
Converge to form one light
Upon a throne, upon a bier;

Or as the roads and cars flow in
To Stratford, and we come
With light of what we have known and been
To lay upon this tomb;
With evening mist and autumn scene.

Love of the Seashore

We come out of a fern-set lane
To tamarisk on the foreshore and
The grass that binds the blond dune sand
And at the ebb a perfect fan,

A coral shell on the furthest beaches
Cast like a dream and soon to fade,
Fall from its salt and pricking shade;
To gulls glassed on their ice-blue stretches,

And to our gull-like outpost stations –
Pouring on pools and waves in trance,
We who are parents, citizens
From neighbourhoods and occupations.

Love of the seashore, lasting faith
So draws us long past infancy,
Past youth, to cape and estuary;
Image of love of sleep not death;

Not love of death, of that full deep
That sluiced from its horizon pours,
The Atlantic soul, to bury ours;
But tidal dailiness of sleep.

Our failure is around us, wrack,
Spoiled picnic, castle trodden over.
Cover with waves our shallows, cover
And drown our world to give it back.

Sleep, rectifying solitude,
Sleep that attunes our daylight faces,
Brother to free and lonely places
Brings marvels also on its flood.

So, these like dreams, sea-wave and shell,
The green-veined blue, the oxblood stone
Come strange with truth beyond our own,
So far-brought, patterned, beautiful,

Come laden to us margin-lovers
Here where we take in hands and sight
All we can bear of infinite;
Haunters of thresholds, gulls and plovers.

Voices in the Evening

The room with darkness filling wide,
Like frost on a ploughed countryside
Pearly on loam of ridges
The light spreads thin on planes and ledges.

Beyond the window children play,
Wild in the fading of the day.
I hear their separate ranging
Unseen, their ritual interchanging,

As if each carried a fire-tipped wand
As the fairies did in the theatre, and
When the stage darkened were
Distilled to fireflies spinning in night air.

These are their air-borne voices light
Earth-linked by less than string of kite
Or tenuous harebell stem,
Yet linked like homing birds each one to one of them.

Song for a Ghost

When or where I cannot guess,
I lost my life in the deep grass
Between youth and middle age,
Not with pain and consciousness
But like a brooch dropped from a dress.

Will the search never be over
Through the trampled grass and clover
Between youth and middle age
Where I slept by hedge and river,
Where I dreamed it was for ever?

While we sleep there's life to lose.
Which of all the flowers I chose
Between youth and middle age
Cupped the poison? Or which grass
Soft of blade was honed to pierce?

When or where I cannot guess,
I lost my life in the deep grass
Between youth and middle age,
Not with pain and consciousness
But like a brooch dropped from a dress.

The Vine at Hampton Court

Nothing is in its house but the great vine
And a skein hung of raffia, large to scale,
And high step-ladder propped on the far wall.

Nothing but the vine in its long house,
And the vine grown its house – all but the rock-
Shaped and clay-coloured, swollen, fantastic stock,

From which the dedicated branches run
Piping their roof's length, held against the sky,
Earth to the leaves, that give them back the sun;

Leaves trained to spread to the utmost, tessellate
Themselves their ceiling, even themselves become
The light that inhabits sole their empty room;

Light fair in colour, filling wall to wall.
For now is spring, the grapes hang high and small.
The tender light, the lucent tree are all.

Spring like a Flood

See how where dry land was the city floats
A swan on lilac now the spring has risen.
My heart marooned (unless we take to boats)
That dark and narrow tower, is twice a prison.
All night I am conscious of the flood round the walls.
At dawn the bird-song rocks them; then a little
Subsiding lets the white reflected halls

And lilac shadows of the rain-clouds settle,
And the day's eye looks over the sheathed water.
All night such images of flowering rise,
Beat on my heart behind its iron shutter
– As the real spring on windows and on eyes
Beats – that that walking dust-storm, tower of stone
And keep of sorrow, almost is brought down.

A Change of Season

The pear blossom has snowed itself away,
Dissolved away over the grass
And over the place where the girl's rug was,
Where in the pith of spring she lay
In the sharp sweetness of her Easter holiday.

These hours we see the clock hands of the year
Move on, these few and heavy hours
When blossom thins and lilac flowers,
And the slate thunder clouds appear
Shadows of lilac trees thrown magnified on air.

Those trees bear such affinity with cloud
That drenched, their depths seem formed of rain,
Their penetralia store that grain;
In the storm's rests they shower abroad
Spray like a blackbird's phrase on hand and sleeve and road.

But the white blossom melts away in grass,
And under the barren cherry tree
Fuller than its reality
The mirror pool on the footpath glows
And swells the gutters with its petal overflows.

On the Beach

Her young boy running ahead, she came through the clefts of rock
And saw him wait in the shallow sea,
Where missing her, in wonder more than anxiety,
He stood and turned his vague eyes back,

And when she came in sight looked away onwards, peace
Fallen on his face, oblivion.
Such fine communications cut like blades of grass,
Bloodless and deep, all but unknown.

Tiger Lilies

The wind disposes shadows of leaves and pears
Over the wall and frieze of flowers.
Shadows of fruit-tree and of pine
Dissolve the lilies' calligraphic line,

And flashing sun puts down their jungle fire;
Till now the sun goes in, and pure
And dark transparence lies like water
Under the trees, and the flame of the flowers burns hotter,

And deeper they incise on darker metals
Their stamens and voluted petals:
On the ripe wall, leaves of anemones,
Of jasmine dense as air, and air conceived for this.

Anxiety in Middle Age

What shall we do, from middle age descending
With our hearts too much demanding
Love or love's shade and empty imitation
Comfort or power or acclamation?
What shall we do with ourselves that cast no shadows,
Young, on the wild and spacious meadows?

Time as it slept in youth fluid and endless,
A sea like space over and round us,
First was betrayed. An enemy came creeping
And touched to stone time's ocean sleeping.
In the light hardening, how worlds stood calcified,
Yet changed, like dreams confirmed yet falsified
By dreams succeeding or by daylight breaking
In a strange room, at a slow waking.

Now fear turns greed, hoarding against calamity –
All fear one fear, of one extremity:
For loss of love we call a kind of dying,
And death dread most as love's untying.
Oh yet, if we could give without demanding
We should not fear love's or life's ending.

Only ourselves to lose, how hard we feel it!
Ourselves to lose, trash in a wallet,
Through all the elaborate ways of loss. Urgently now beseeches
Even the dove clothed in the beeches.

The River Steamer

Waiting for a spirit to trouble the water.

Waiting for a spirit from beneath or over
To trouble the surface of the river
From which the hours like clouds reflected gaze
White, and the daylight shines of all earth's days,

Waiting for a spirit to dissolve the glass,
I see, in the unbreaking wave that fans from us,
Incline and circle the reeds and sedges;
And see the ripples on the under sides of bridges

And under the dark green leaves of deepest summer
And the green awning of the river steamer,
The secondary ripple, the shadow's shadow,
Abstract and pure appearance, follow and follow;

And see the roan banks flecked with rose and seed
Of willow herb, and fields beside the river-bed
Freshened by total light in day's decline,
And the elms standing in the heart of the sun;

And hear the passengers telling the day's praises,
And the tired wildness of their children's voices
Too young for the journey's hours; and all of these
Clear in the river's glass, I also praise,

Waiting for a spirit to transpierce the glaze.

Fire of Spring

Thin fire throughout the wood
Lays a pale pewter burnish
On undergrowth of hazel
And still drifts of the elder
That light and lichen tarnish,

And seem to pour through these
As water through its falling
In stone-smooth weirs and rapids –
So fast through woods in stillness
The spies of fire are filing.

The blue of a true flower
Shines from field ruts and furrows –
Not winter skies in water
Nor light on leaves of ivy,
Nor any blue earth borrows

From air; nor (dreamed through trees
A lake as blue as lacquer)
Wood smoke; but flowers of speedwell
Rooted in sheltering hoof-prints
And valleys of the tractor.

River Scene

This day as blue as whey, this milk-blue day,
Hardly distinguishing air from their stream
The swans upon the kerchief river
Take easily to the pale sky over,
Blue bleached to almost white, as deep as light.

The aerial waters make themselves a lake,
The lake a sea, and that, infinity.
The swans dispart the depth and shining,
Floating or flying, poised or turning;
In realms of abstract bloom possessed, at home.

Visit to a Child at Night

Why so still, so wide awake, cold face
And bird-in-bramble eyes coloured with dark's darkness?
The little light, that entering I let in
From distant turns of stair, draws whiteness from your skin
As even moonless nights from waterfalls
And tracts of flood and heart-shaped pools.

Then were you watching night, so quiet I took you
For long asleep, or did my tread on carpet wake you?
Or do your eyes, as black as new-born, blind
Gaze from another night and hemisphere of mind?
If this is sleep I fear to rouse you, speaking.
Speak to me first if this is waking.

Though we seem met by flood or heart-shaped pool,
By less than moonlight or the moon invisible,
Caught to a zone of mysteries and dangers,
It is not for the first time and we are not strangers.
I say your name. Who should it be but I?
Asleep or waking, you reply.

Invocation to a Poem

Condense like light on the branch of a cold tree.
It lies as still as a lynx on the level bough,
The neutral and gentle daylight of the world;
And primrose buds in the hazel mould
Of many woods and seasons condense there now,

And mist there gathers its haunting from many mornings
And stands between the branches. Out of air
Condense and fall, as light or memory
Or flocks of starlings fall to a tree;
As the birds close in to rest for a night-time there.

Swarm like the birds on a tree or shine as light
From surface of bark or leaf, water or metal,
Or like remembered springs draw in to a small
Pattern of boughs through a window. All
Creation is yours; but elect and gather and settle.

Sorrows of Childhood

Your griefs lie where they fall to earth.
Do you remember now your hamster's death? –
That died at night, no one to know,
Claiming at last its lost wild status so.

That death was altered when you cried.
Now it is in your hands the hamster died;
And in my head your fondling moan,
Though it was brief in time, sounds on and on.

Your griefs lie where they fall to ground.
You on your forward way do not look round.
Slighter, and yet incurable,
Your griefs in me, the ground on which they fall.

Walking into Yew Woods

The ribbon-leaved grass is in seed
In clearings and by paths, the blade
And loose grain bowed, grace to remember,
Printed on deep or broken shade
Or violet-flowering glades in full September.

But far in the yew wood soil is dry,
Kind, soft as dust; the dropped twigs lie.
The obdurate trunks keep, sandstone-red,
A bloom, a shade of shade of sky
Darkening. Alone here I should be afraid.

Alone here I should be afraid.
You are my innocence. Alone I should
Sink under hauntings I'd encounter here
Or bring here. Now they give the wood
Only an edge on peace, an autumn frost of fear.

The Enclosed Valley

A quarry blocks the pathway to the valley
There where it would emerge.
The stream above is squandered under sedge
Or sleeps deep under bracken fronds
Where once the Britons carved their seven ponds;
The spring is tree-roofed and secluded wholly.

Now down the hill-side is the only way there
By rampart or by fosse
Stick-strewn and stony as a dry flood course
By bramble and by nettle bed
With thorn and vaulted elder overhead
And leaves of ash breaking far off on daylight;

And at the hill-foot, welcome beyond hope,
Marsh-green and flowered a lawn
Stems the stream's wandering. Here they came down
For water in the time before
The woods were these, or yet the unhistoried war
Had filled the long grave on the further slope.

Peace now is here afterwards as before;
Here more than elsewhere. Sparse
The harebell flowers, and under leaves and grass
The spring throbs still, clogged and diminished.
Nothing unchanged, nothing is wholly finished.
But peace is here; such tides have drenched this shore.

Freezing Point

Water will freeze tonight
Under the North wind –
The surface water that no more
Drops its cold weight to the lake floor
But stretched prepares to die
Under the air's hand.

And on its stiffening sheen
Under the North wind
From the crown-large flamingo sun
Such ashen colours are borne down
As seem to bloom upon
No water but wastes of sand.

So wide the lake becomes
At year's and day's end,
And looks towards its glaciation
Like one who waits a change of state
Remote from our compassion
Under the North wind.

Hyacinth

So near symmetrical,
A flower-book diagram almost,
Calling for praise before its small
Perfection is outgrown and lost.

We make it live to please:
It does please, following its stars,
Unfolding flowers as cream as cheese,
Spacing its leaves to mime a vase

As upheld fingers might
When sun through rose capillaries shines.
Through this green blood the winter light,
Clouded, silvers the lengthwise lines.

The Stream Bank

All strands that reach it the stream turns,
Brambles and grass, to figures in its motion.
The ash tree keeps its perfect clear relation
To water and reflected suns.

Air through the many-hanging flowered and ferny
Curtaining of the deep-set stream
Moves it to imitate the pulse and beam
Of the fragile water's journey.

The grass heads, filled with air-like fountains pause
Over their drenched green – blade and moss,
And those least flowers that take the grass
For cover and for sky, stars in its space –

Till water, air and hanging meadows seem
Of one continuous substance, each
So fixed in flowing, and the touch
Seems deft and light of time creating them.

Times of Life

No longer the unbridled crying near or far
Of little children calls me – their archaic voices,
I know they are not mine – whose learned weeping presses
Like ours against a heavy door,

Who are not always near, in the lap, in the house's hollow,
In the cradle mind; but free among the circling flocks
Now write on field and street invisible their tracks,
Paths in the air of lark or swallow.

My thought dwells on those trails, picks out and silvers them.
But the cries of infants knock, and yet must house elsewhere –
From road or neighbouring garden filling a world of air
Like wail of lambs from a mountain stream.

Agnostic

I have lived my life long
With one who cannot speak a word,
Or if a word, not of my tongue
More than sound of stream or bird;
Or if of my tongue, unheard.

I am deaf or this is dumb,
This life and world apart from me
To whom betrothed at birth I came,
In whose silence most I see
A calling soul, calling my scrutiny.

So where deepest silence lies
Gathered to pools, my steps will draw:
The speechless child that sleeps or cries;
Age with the secret, not the power;
The look of utterance on the silent flower.

You with religious faith, to whom
Life speaks in words you understand –
Believe, I also with my dumb
Stranger have made a marriage bond
As strong and deep and torturing and fond.

Trees in Rain

Heavy as if they held their fruit
The trees are filled with rain.
The chestnuts stand – though bearing
Already all they can,
Their utmost leaves and flowering –
Hooded in water head to foot,
And gusts drive now and then
Before the blind face of the beeches
A smoke of houseless rain.

These garden forms gentle and large
Through which the pigeons strike
Upwards to clefts beyond,
Where light in foam must break
Shattered on foliage –
These that hold summer in one hand
Now with the other take
Wildness, the world's inclemency,
Like birds into their ark.

Winter Daylight

O light, our bread! Familiar in the room
The winter daylight is diffused and pearly,
Fallen through clouds of snow; and so far come
Settles on walls and chair and hands and hair; the early
Sky-coloured crocuses reflect it nearly.

The girl stooped to the fire wears on her green
Shoulder the window's light, a feather of
The swan that claps and stretches wings again
Over us, giving us our own, and power to move
Us by their forms giving to all we love.

Manqué

Well, Truth, I am your slave. To Love I give what I can,
But I was bound to you before my life began.
Love and fear of my lord, with love of Love, from youth
Confused me. Both betrayed, forgive me, Love and Truth.

A Distant View of Parnassus

So, it is true, they are not gentle,
The Muses, hardly if at all
Accessible. Their mountain wall
Offers no hold to root or tendril.
Seeds of pansies, rock rose, even
Parnassus grass might strike and fall
From cliffs so gaunt, high, virginal,
So harsh to earth, so locked with heaven.

A Dream Forgotten

As I woke from a harrowing dream,
Fifty years old in me the habit of waking said:
"Loosen it; it is a dream.
Open your hand; you need not unwind the coils in the thread.
The lost need not be found, the truth need not be told.
Release your hold."

So as the waker must
I did, and out of sleep fell into dreamless waking.
That iron fabric passed
Frail out of mind as foam on sand, the clear domes breaking;
Faster than sound or light, faster than anything known,
Covering its tracks, was gone.

With relief on a cool
Shore stranded, yet I strained towards the dark where the harsh
      dream went.
It was a world and full
As any world of sorrow, fear, bewilderment.
Yet it bore life, and interest was its circling breeze,
And pearls enhanced its seas.

If to die should be so –
To hear: "It is a dream; let it go" and loose as we must
The unknown that's all we know –
Even in oblivion I should mourn a whole world lost.
Signs dark to understand, pearls never dived for yet
I should find means to regret.

VI
Translations from the Italian of Giovanni Pascoli (1855-1912)

Pascoli often refers in his poems (sometimes explicitly, sometimes only by tone) to the great unhappiness of his late childhood and adolescence. His father was murdered when Giovanni was eleven years old, and his mother, two brothers and a sister died in the following few years. The reader needs to know this in order to understand some of the poems, such as "The Meteor".

November

The air so spangled, sun so brilliant,
You turn towards the apricots to find
A flower there still, and the whitethorn's bitter scent
        Rises in your mind.

But dry the thorn, the trees are stark as dead;
With their black mesh they score the empty air.
Earth underfoot sounds hollow to the tread
        And the sky is bare

And silence everywhere; only in gusts
From distant gardens where the leaves are shed
You hear the fragile falling. Time of ghosts,
        Cold summer of the dead.

They are Ploughing

In the morning fields, where fiery red a spray
Of vine still burns in the hedge-row, and from bushes
The early mist like smoke is flowing away,

They are ploughing: one man urging on the slow
Cattle, slow-voiced, one sowing, one who pushes
The clods of earth back with his patient hoe.

And all they do the knowing sparrow watches,
Feasting in fancy, from its bramble hold,
And the robin sees, and out of woods and hedges
Sends its slight tinkling song that shines like gold.

Carter

Carter, who have come from your black mountain ridges
Untroubled to our dales, though all the night
You were under hanging cliffs, on airy bridges,

Tell us what the voice of the north wind said,
Lowing in gulleys, wailing on the height. –
But you were sleeping on your charcoal bed.

Hour after hour upon the mountain way
The storm wind passed whistling and wild along.
But in your dream it spoke of Christmas day.
You heard the Christmas pipers raise their song.

Romagna
(To Severino)

Always one village, always, haunting me,
One inward landscape smiles, or mourns, Severino.
However far you journey there, you see
Still the blue phantom peak of San Marino.

This is my countryside, where the Malatesta
And Guidi reigned, and with his desperadoes
The bold and gentle Ferryman was master,
King of the highroads and the forest shadows.

There in the stubble where the turkey hen
Goes sobbing with her foster brood, by the glittering
Light on the pool and the scattered water when
The slow ducks with their rainbow heads are weltering –

Oh, if we could be there, lost in green cover!
Or standing by the elms, the nest of the jay,
Could shout and hear our voices, carried over
The mid-day drowsing farms, die far away,

146

Where the bent labourer raises his head
And lays his sickle down and lifts his bowl,
And the tired cattle dream in peace and shade,
Munching their sainfoin in the dusk of the stall;

And from far villages we'd hear the bell –
Tower beyond tower, that with their silver cries
Call to cool shelter, call to quiet, call
To where the table flowers with children's eyes.

Once, at my home, an acacia tree would spread us
Its lacy sunshade for these scorching hours.
All summer long it gave its leaves to shade us
And filled our eyes with its rosy feathered flowers;

And close beside it, by the crumbling wall,
Thick-set and dense with leaves a rose tree held
A jasmine in its arms, and over all
A poplar chattered like a noisy child.

This was my nest, and dreaming there I rode
With Guidon Selvaggio or Astolfo far
Across the hills; or there before me stood,
Pale in his Hermitage, the Emperor.

And while I fought with heroes, while I soared
High with the Hippogriff in dreams of glory,
Or in the silence of my room I heard
Exiled Napoleon dictate his story,

I would hear through all, where the hay lay freshly mown,
The crickets' song perpetually quiver,
And from their brooks I would hear the frogs intone
Their wordless poem that goes on for ever.

And long and endless poems without words,
Foreshadowings and dreams of poems, came to me:
Rustle of summer leaves, piping of birds,
Laughter of women, roaring of the sea.

This was our nest; but on a bitter day
We flew, late swallows, from the home of our birth.
My country now is where I live, but they
Had not so far to go; they were laid in the earth.

So I shall never come again through your hazy
Mornings, your dusty hawthorn lanes, to where
My nest lay deep in leaves – for fear the lazy
Cuckoo has come and left her fledgelings there –

My loved Romagna, where the Malatesta
And Guidi reigned, and with his desperadoes
The bold and gentle Ferryman was master,
King of the highroads, king of the shadows.

Rain

From farm to farm the cock in darkness called.

And the rook in the wood croaked from its nest.
The sun appeared in every window pane
And over waste and scrub gilded the mist;
Then hid away, and there came floods of rain.
Then, with the tree-frogs' chorusing, again
A long and yellow ray flashed on the world.

The summer swallow-broods were struck with wonder
By that fine fall of needles through the air;
The rush of rain with its gentle gulping under;
The mottled ground, the drumming everywhere;
Then sobbing, and the drops then few and rare,
Sprinkled in crystal cups, the drops of gold.

The Hedge

(A section of a long poem about country people)

I

Hedge of my holding, faithful and benign,
Rounding this garden like the wedding ring
That names as mine the woman who is mine

(And I your husband proud and flourishing,
Gentle dark earth, ready to love and please
The tyrant with his burnished harrowing)

Hedge, keeping out with your intricacies
The daytime-drowsy thief, welcoming all
Nest-building birds and grazing swarms of bees;

Hedge I repaired and strengthened like a wall
As still the household grew – re-planted part,
Every day happier, richer not at all;

Of hawthorn, tamarisk and pomegranate
With honeysuckle scent flowing between:
Through you I am rich and lord of my estate,

Hedge of my holding, city-wall of green.

II

How wise you are! – If thirsty travellers
Come by you offer berries for their pleasure,
But save the fruit-trees with their dangling pears.

You bring no gifts towards the housewife's treasure,
Her hoarded jars; but happy in your care
She reaps the laden cherry-trees at leisure.

You bring no gifts, and yet the vines declare
(When by the track I prune them, and the voice
Of the cuckoo from the hill is in the air) –

Declare: "You are our father; as you choose
You rule, and guide us through the poplar maze.
But the hedge is the mother who takes care of us."

149

"Through her I have oil and wine for all my days"
I answer. From the yard the cocks call too,
Applauding, and the watch-dog barks his praise –

Who is a voice, my silent hedge, to you.

III

And yet you do speak briefly in your turn,
Mute at the boundary, giving the world
A prohibition sharper than a thorn;

Giving consent, like flowers, within the fold;
Hedge firm to others, but to me benign,
Like the faith given with a ring of gold

That names as mine the woman who is mine.

Mistletoe

I

Then do you not remember now the bloom
Of those marvellous mornings? They were clouds in our sight,
The pink of the peach blossom, the white of the plum,

And all the air spangled with flakes, all white
Or pink or both: apple trees, sturdy pears,
Delicate apricots, all hung with light.

So blurred we saw that garden through our tears
Dazzling us, and for days it held the sky's
Bright unexpected dawn mirrored for us.

And that was hope, those days were promises.
But the bees already streaming from their hives
Were feeding on illusion; for of this

They make, like me, the honey of their lives.

II

A cloud, a shower of rain...so winter came
Back by degrees, and for dreary days we kept
Indoors and listened to the muttering flame.

The white and rosy trees had vanished, steeped
In constant fog, and through the sallow air
A never-ending hiss of spindles crept.

It rained and rained. The sun then (sprung from where?)
Once more with the church bells' ringing rose and shone.
The world was green, green lay our garden there.

Where were the filigree clusters? All gone,
The petals all on the ground. We trod our vain
Memories under foot in the light of the dawn,

Each memory laden with its tears again.

III

I said – you remember? – "Sister of my soul,
They are living things; and you know for life we choose
To throw away what is more beautiful

Even than life itself, for life to lose
Our fragile spring. See, the tree that has found
A thousand thirsty apples on its boughs

Still points to the flowers it yielded to the ground...
But not" – I checked myself – "that strange tree there
That has no fruit nor any petals round."

It stood beyond the reach of joy or fear,
That tree, it had no winter and no spring –
Stripped by the early rain-storms of the year

Only of leaves, that are born for scattering.

IV

I said (do you remember?): "Nameless tree,
Unnatural tree with leaves whose colours clash,
Two green shoots and one yellowish, strange to see;

Poor wretched tree whose branches do not match,
Nor yet your leaves, some of them pointed, some
Rounded; and then such evil beads and such

Sinister ravelled webs; poor tree, infirm
And sickly tree, never to bear a flower
Nor see your wings blown down in any storm;

Dead tree, indifferent to the gentle air
Bringing the pollen, and the rain whirled through
The garden beds, lashing the vines...For sure

The roots of the mistletoe are fast in you.

V

What wind of hatred brought it to you? – dark
Enemy power, or blind, implanted you?
The small soft seed lay in your iron bark.

You did not know, or would not think it true.
It was his will: he made your life his food,
With his green veins he ploughed your marrow through.

You languished, and the beautiful and good
Passed from your mind, and never more you sent
Your buds out throbbing through your mossy wood.

He throve, he conquered; and your colours went,
And all the flowing sweetness of your prime –
Your apples with their juice, flowers with their scent –

Is shrunken to a pallid pearl of slime.

Two souls are in you, tree. Do you feel their war
Still? Do you hear them still as you brood and sway
In the dreamy surge and murmur of the air?

The one that could be desolate or gay,
That smiled with the opening lips of buds in you
And wept in you when your shoots were pruned away,

That shook with passion as the hive bees flew –
That earlier soul, you have forgotten her,
Or she, herself. You have become the new,

And fly, fly without motion, more and more
Fly from yourself. Yet the shadow on your hearth
Is you. Whatever blossom once you bore,

It is you who now press out the gum of death."

The Kite

There is something new today in the bright air,
New and yet old. I am in a different mood
And place, and smell the violets in flower.

They are in flower in the monastery wood,
In the Capuchins' school, under the brown
Of leaves the wind stirs at the oak-tree's foot.

And the air, sweet to breathe, is breaking down
The hardened clods of earth and visiting
Countryside churches with their steps grass-grown;

An air of a different place, a different spring,
A different life from this; a sky-blue air
That holds a flock of white shapes hovering –

Our kites are up, yes, soaring high and far.
For this is a holiday. We trooped between
Hedges of blackberry and hawthorn here.

The hedges all were spined and bare; no green,
But here and there a few of autumn's red
Berries in clusters, or a white flower shone

Of spring. A robin hopped and pivoted
On a bare branch; a lizard through the dry
Leaves in the ditch poked up its little head.

And this is where we stop, in sight of high
Windy Urbino – all of us now vying
To launch our comets on the turquoise sky.

There it goes, wavering, colliding, dying –
And lifts, and takes the wind. Oh, there at last,
Through the long yell from the throats of the boys, it is flying.

Flying; from our hands snatching its string so fast,
It seems a flower in flight on its thin stem,
Escaped to flower again on another coast.

Flying; and the breathless lungs and face aflame
And trembling legs of the child, and heart, and eyes –
Into the sky it is sweeping all of them.

Higher, still higher! A bright dot, it flies
So high, a shining spark. Oh, but a wind
Sidelong, a cry... Whose voice is it that cries?

I know them all, the voices of that band;
Strange how across the years I know them well,
One sweet, one shrill, one muffled and low-toned.

And one by one again I see you all,
My school-friends; and you with them, you whose white
Face on a shoulder drooping lay so still.

I said the prayers over you, at night
I cried for you. Yet you were happiest.
The wind brought down for you only a kite.

It is your whiteness I remember best,
And how your knees kept still a trace of red
From our long praying where the floor had pressed.

Oh, you were happiest, who went to bed
Clasping your favourite toy, and closed your eyes
And followed easily where you were led.

For death is surely kind to one who dies
Clasping his childhood, as a flower unblown
Keeps folded its white petals where it lies

Cut off in bud. Oh, dead in childhood, soon
I shall be coming too under the earth
Where you have slept in peace so long alone.

Better to come there rosy, out of breath
And warm with sweat – straight from the open air
And the race to the hill-top, better to come to death.

Better to come there with your head still fair.
For you, when you lay cold upon the sheet,
It was your mother combed your wavy hair,

Gently so that you were not hurt by it.

The Fallen Oak

Where its shade lay, now the oak lies on the grass
Dead, no more wrestling with the wind. They say:
We really see it now. How tall it was!

The laden nests of spring hang as they may
Scattered among the branches of its crown.
We see it now. How kind it was! they say.

They praise, they cut their faggots; night comes down,
They leave, with heavy bundles strapped behind.
A voice in the air... A bird calls on and on,

Looking for the nest it will not find.

The Book

I

High in the gallery on its oak stand
The book is open. When the oak tree stood
Alive and buffeted by the north wind,

When it was still in leaf in its loud wood,
The book was old already. Open now,
It hears the beetles boring for their food.

And someone has come in, it seems – but how?
Not through the wavering curtain at the door
Where winds from the mountain and the desert blow,

Suddenly risen; yet comes, and stands before
The book and turns the leaves – this I can tell
From their soft swish; I cannot see him, where

I hear him like a thought, invisible.

II

Someone is there, who leafing through the book
Runs quickly from the first page to the last,
Then from the last to the first more slowly back.

And caught in the fury of his fruitless quest
Over and over the fragile pages turn,
Twenties and hundreds in his fuming fist;

Then slowly, lingeringly, one by one,
A little while; then fast again, and more
Frantically, page on page he slams them down;

And stops. Has he found it? The creaking of the door
Dies, and the world sways in pure silence. Then,
Is he reading it? He is searching as before,

Through the warped leaves he is hunting truth again.

III

And still he is searching, while the evening blooms
Red out of clouds; and drifting thunder strays;
And through a fluttering like phantoms' plumes.

And still he is searching while the shadows raise
Their swelling tents in the wind, and soon come over
The constellations on their desert ways

And sacred night is here. Still and for ever.
I catch, through all, the leaves' dry rustling,
Though in the sky the songs of sirens hover.

For ever, through the voices wandering,
I hear him like a thought, invisibly
Backwards and forwards leafing and questioning

Under the stars, the book of mystery.

The Hearth

I

Night; and at times flashes of lightning, showing
Travellers lost, wandering in wind and snow,
Past telling how they came or where they are going.

But darkness drinks them; far away they go –
Walking alone, or holding by the hand
An image of themselves, whose pace is slow.

And some keep empty eyes upon the ground;
Some turn them in a dream of voices; some
Upraise them to the clouds and spaces round;

And some are weeping, some walk fierce and dumb.

II

But most are weeping, though their sorrow passes
Unheard. Round every one of them the air
Is full of other grief that no-one guesses.

But each sees shining in the lightning's glare
A cottage, set alone in the barren land;
And in his heart each of them murmurs: "There

At least I can rest awhile." From wandering and
Bewilderment, through the dark air they come
To the open cottage door; and now they stand

Before the house, where no-one is at home.

III

Unknown to one another still, unseen
They have come from the four winds to this dumb fold;
And one by one in silence they go in.

"Here it is not so desolate and cold"
Under their breath they say, between their sighs;
And sit by the wall there, sheltered from the world.

Beyond the wall they hear the fury rise
Of all the sky, and feel the fear of earth
And tremble, hidden from each other's eyes

In darkness... Yet, in the midst of them, a hearth.

IV

Lightning from time to time reveals these mourning
Wanderers waiting with their still hands crossed
Before the hearth, on which no fire is burning –

Till one by one they come to hear the fast
Beating of other hearts, and find at their side
A listening ear, a speaking voice, at last

And the old man by the child, white by rose-red,
The woman by the man, entrustingly
Each on a stranger's shoulder rests his head,

His heavy head, worn out by mystery.

V

And now the spell-binder begins to talk;
And his bright fable hangs and throws its beams
Over their heads, a lamp lit in the dark,

Hour after hour; till every listener dreams
The thin, faint echo of a flame is lit
On the cold hearth – a ghost of fire-light gleams;

Till none of them is weeping where they sit
By the cold hearth, nor shuddering at the weather
Now; they have warmth; no fire created it.

It is the comfort of their being together.

VI

Stretching their hands some stoop towards the flames
With hearts at peace, and in a pose of prayer
Outspread together seem their open palms.

The young ones, happy now, without a care
Draw round the empty hearth in unison,
Cheered by the fragile flame that is not there.

Mothers of children have one hand alone
Stretched to the fire; the other is behind
On a blonde head. Even grief takes sweetness on

In the bare cottage battered by the wind.

VII

Even sweet is the darkness of the common fate
We share by the dead hearth. Yet there are some
Who leave the roof and voice and empty grate

And go their strange and desperate ways. The storm
Bitter in heart and tongue breaks on their heads.
And of its words some reach the quiet room

Where these keep watch; where the black weather rides
Over their gentle souls entranced in faith,
Rapt in the dream the story-teller sheds,

While all around them cries the voice of death.

Vertigo

(Spoken by a boy who has lost his belief in gravitation)

I

Humans, I look at you, and in my mind
Springs fear; I cannot move or make a sound.
I see you hang in the never-ending wind.

I see you with your helpless feet on the ground,
On the stones or grass of our world astray and floating.
You hang with emptiness below you and round.

Oh, think, you are not trees anchored by rooting –
That only spread and fling their branches wide
As far in the sky as in earth they fix their footing.

You are not like the sea, held high and tied
Fast in its place by an upward wind that flows
From the sky below and is never modified.

The sea must thrust its waves without a pause
Towards night, from which answering perpetually
Its harsh and broken voice, the light wind blows.

But you – who holds your feet firm where they lie?
You go your ways, narrowing your thoughts and sight
To this uncouth, flying obscurity;

With chin on chest, muffled against the light,
Clogged by denial and oblivion –
And hanging, you who think you walk upright!

But when you lift your eyes, when you lean down
Over the gulf where at the end of all,
So deep, so far, the fires of Vega shine –

Why, then I fling my hands and clutch a wall,
A rock, or tree, or blade of grass, in my
Terror of space – or nothing real at all

On earth, for fear I should fall into the sky.

II

Oh but the night! If it were never night!
To hang above those cold (cold as my fears)
Those far-off shining, blue and red and white –

Over that infinite abyss of stars,
Over that host, over that million,
That scattering of seed, sandstorm of stars.

Over that infinite abyss you run
Yet never cross it, Earth; and carry us
Hung from your rocks in blind oblivion.

But I keep watch, and the wind of your course
Blows in my heart. I watch; with its eyes wide
The Great Bear into mine all the night stares.

But if I should let go, and slip, and slide,
And all my being plunge in that dark well
Of worlds, that sea with no returning tide...

Moment by moment to watch brightening all
The constellations and the drifting stars,
And the great sky enlarging as I fall;

To fall dissolved in weakness, faint with fears,
And to be nothing, weightless, bodiless,
And every moment fall a thousand years;

And deeper down than all I see, or guess,
To reach no ground; never to pause or halt
From one to another solitude of space;

Perhaps, beyond, beyond, to hope for... what?
Stillness; an end; the finish of the road?
For you to hope, for you, I, whirled about

From sky to sky, in vain, for ever, God!

The Servant Girl from the Mountains

All of them out, all of them gone.
Timid and wild, the girl from the hills
Left in the kitchen sits alone.
The copper pans hang on the walls.
Her eyes roam all about her, then
Fall to her lap again.

Nothing familiar round,
Nothing she knows; all dark and dumb
Looms to her sight. And not a sound
But when the flies on the window hum;
But for the low and inward clucking
The pot on the fire is making.

A sharp mouse-muzzle comes
And goes at a crack, and comes once more.
The water heating on the flames
Changes its note and rings... From far,
Farther away than heart can tell
The sound falls of a bell...

Of a mule on the mountain track –
Higher and higher, on and on
Between the distant small and black
Beech-trees climbing, seen and gone;
Only the swaying bell at its neck
Sounds on without a break.

Still an hour of day to come.
In the blue air the moon is a flake.
How lovely to be journeying home
Through the long evening, still not dark.
One of those days that never end,
And the scents of summer round.

The far-off singing bell
Is almost lost in all she hears;
Lost in the mountain waterfall
There at her feet, filling her ears,
And in the constant changing breeze
Through the full leaves of the trees.

She hears the nightingale
Singing, now other birds are dumb,
Alone, alone but for the owl,
Tuning for her watch to come,
That will end when morning breaks
At the chiming of the larks.

Nightfall

Through evening's beauty, worlds draw near.
The sky and earth are close and talk.
In the clear air a star:
A lamp here in the dark.

Creatures of earth and sky converse
As earth grows dark, so gradually
Time passing seems to pause
Waiting for what will be.

Three planets in their blue abysses:
Three windows bordering the dim river.
In the hushed town, seven houses:
Seven Pleiades hung over.

Black houses: white are the broods of stars.
Scattered houses: Algol, Sirius...
A star or group of stars
For each man or tribe of us.

And each a world, each of those houses
Holds fire within that shines abroad,
And shelters laughing voices
By passers-by unheard.

Between the worlds, a veil of grey,
Smoke clouds from all the chimneys stream:
Above, the Milky Way
Drifts through the quivering calm.

The Meteor

So late, under the bright, dark height of the sky
In all the length of road no soul but I
Moved, and the Salto flowing silently.

I could not hear the stream, but from its banks
I heard its escort frogs that in their ranks
Call: Water, Water, for the fields and tanks.

Twenty years old, graceless, my memory
Too full of pain, I dreamed of more to be,
A bloody death prepared also for me.

And yet at night alone I had to take
The shadowed road where the enemy might lurk.
My steps were soft and slow and my heart shook.

He would not see my fear, where he was lying,
Though I would tremble at a beetle flying
Suddenly, or the wind shifting and sighing.

My steps were soft and slow, my heart raced on.
What will it be? A blow, a whirling down,
And on the road to die in pain alone...

No, not alone. The graveyard is close by
With its dim lamp that burns perpetually.
My mother would come running at my cry.

Though she would barely touch me with her hand,
Her tears, as light as dew shed on the ground
In darkness, I would feel upon my wound.

The others would come too, crying in thin
Faint voices, and would lift and take me in,
And in their country they would heal my pain –

Country of consolation, where you are laid
To sleep and smile for ever on a bed
Woven of grass and moss, as nests are made.

So as I walked in dreams and heard at the edge
Of the road, by that great elm, beyond the hedge,
Beyond the vines, a whispered word, savage,

A flash, a burst... Oh, there upon the night
Burst, shone, fell, fell, had fallen, through the light
Of stars, from the unimaginable height,

A globe of gold, that dived without a sound,
Was quenched as if in cloud in the empty land;
Yet lit for its one moment, far around,

Hedges and furrows, cottages, the floods
Of wandering rivers and the stationed woods,
And the white towns massed at the ends of roads.

I cried "Oh look!" – my soul caught over me.
But the sky shone; no eyes on earth to see,
Foot-steps, nor shadow of humanity;

The sky alone; and through its darkness shed
The light of its great stars was round my head,
So that I knew I was of Earth indeed,

And Earth, of the sky; she too of the universe;
And saw myself below, how small I was,
And lost, upon a star journeying through stars.

The Song of the Olives

I

Against the castle stones
That ivy and rough brambles cover,
Where the brown hawk will nest and hover
And nothing lives but these

(And the hawk screams and lifts
And settles, circling down the sky,
When the old bailiff passes by
Who holds the castle keys)

Against that hate that in the end
Is left with its own ruins round,
We plant our olive trees:

II

The olives that will give
Their fruit to be our light and food
And feed the mountain thrush's brood
Out of their plenty too;

The olives that will cool
With grey-green shade the scorching rocks
Where the sheep stray and lose their flocks
And the lamb calls the ewe;

And if the son of man should pass
Riding upon his patient ass,
Will offer boughs to strew.

III

Bring only pickaxes;
The plough leave in the idle yard.
This ground rejects mattock and spade –
These shelving terraces,

This steep and barren slope
Oppressed by the cicada's song –
That drunk with sun sings all day long–
And white with rocks and screes.

Here let them grow; they need no more
To root and grow, than sun and air
And time, our olive trees.

IV

Anchored in stone, in air
Their little silver leaves put forth.
Then save for trees of weaker growth
The softer valley soil.

This tree will use what earth
Is given, and bear what weather comes;
Rock-rooted, will not fall in storms
While the rocks do not fall;

And out of poverty it blesses
And from the hardest earth it presses
The softest balm of all.

V

To please ourselves, we sowed
Our flaxen cornfields quick to ripen,
After one winter's snow to open
Under one summer's breeze;

And set fast-growing trees,
Laurels, to spread their branches over
By the ephemeral singing river –
Only ourselves to please;

Wisely; but now, food for our children,
Now shelter for our children's children,
We plant our olive trees.

VI

You, fast-maturing trees,
Yield us return of shade and fruit,
Then comfort for a winter's night,
The murmuring short-lived flame.

From you, pale tree of peace,
We ask for nothing now; but live;
But safely, slowly, grow and thrive
Through still unspoken time;

But nurse the light that will be shed,
Alone will watch above the bed
In our last quiet room.

The Sound of the Pipes

(In Advent, shepherds came down from the hills before dawn and played a traditional tune before shrines of the Virgin.)

I heard in my sleep the pipers tuning.
I heard their lullay an hour before morning.
Through all the sky the stars are shining.
In all the cottages lights are burning.

The shepherds have come so far from the darkened
Folds of their mountains down to us here.
Behind the cottage walls they have wakened
All the good people, simple and poor.

Now under the beam they light the wick –
All of them yawning, heavy from bed.
Those lights are laden with sleep and dark
And hush of talking and weight of tread.

Those votive lanterns everywhere burning,
Here at the window, there by the wall,
Have made of the world, an hour before morning,
A candle-lit crib as vast as small.

The stars through all the dark sky shining
Seem stilled to listen from far in space;
And now in the valley the pipes, beginning,
Lift up their melting voices of peace:

Voices of peace in church or cell,
Voices of home and the children sleeping,
The mother singing; voices of all
Our lost, assuaging, causeless weeping.

O pipers, come from the years before
The day, before reality:
Now while the stars are bright in the air
Watching our transient mystery,

While no-one yet has laid the meal,
While no-one yet has lit the fire,
Before the bells begin to peal,
Give us your leave to weep an hour.

Not now without a cause, with a host
Of causes; yes; but the heart demands
That flood of crying that then is past,
That storm of sorrow that breaks and ends.

Still it desires that innocent rain
Over its new, real torments and fears;
Over its pleasure, over its pain
Prays for those far-off reasonless tears.

Mist

Cover what is far,
White of mist, drifting high,
Flowing over the brightening
Of daybreak in the sky,
After the night-long lightning
And the rock-falls in the air.

Cover what is gone.
Hide the dead from me.
Let me see no more than the tall
Hedge at my boundary,
And where, in the cracks of the wall,
Are the roots of valerian.

Cover what is dead.
The world is drunk with grief.
Let me see my fruit trees only
Deep in flower and leaf –
That give their golden honey
For my bitter bread.

Cover what is far.
Cover the love of the dead.
Let me see, for all their calling,
Only the white of the road.
In time, to the bells' tolling,
I shall go where they are.

Cover what is far.
Hide it away from me.
Let me see, of all beyond,
Only one cypress tree;
With my garden, near at hand,
And my dog drowsing there.

The Weaver

I come to the bench in front of the loom,
Just as I used to in years out of mind.
She, as she used to, moves to make room
In front of the loom.
And never a sound, no word at all.
Only her smile comes, gentle and kind.
Her white hand lets the shuttle fall.

With tears I ask: How could I have gone?
How could I have left you, my long-desired?
Silent she answers with tears alone:
How could you have gone?
And draws towards her, sadly and slow,
The silent comb; and never a word.
Silent the shuttle flies to and fro.

With tears I ask: Why does it not sing,
The treble comb, as it did long ago?
Gentle she echoes me, wondering:
Why does it not sing?
And: O my love – says, weeping, weeping –
Have they not told you? Do you not know?
I have no life now but in your keeping.

Dead, I am dead, yes; weaving, I weave
In your heart only. So it must be
Till wrapped in this sheet at last, my love,
I sleep by you, near the cypress tree.

Night-Flowering Jasmine

And the flowers of night unfold in the hour
When I remember those
I love. And moths of dusk appear
In the heart of the guelder rose.

An end has come to calls and songs;
Only one house hums on.
The nests are sleeping under wings
As eyes under their lids drawn down.

Out of the open cups of the flowers
Their strawberry scent is shed.
The light shines in the wakeful house.
The grass springs on graves of the dead.

By the full hive loiterers buzz,
Late stragglers at the door.
The Hen leads out her brood of stars
Over the dark-blue threshing-floor.

All night the scent wells from the flowers
And the wind scatters it.
The lamp is carried up the stairs,
Shines at a window and goes out.

And morning comes; the flowers fold.
The crumpled petals brood,
Enclosed in their soft, secret world,
What strange and new beatitude?

The Woodmen's Friend

The foreign woodmen, slow to talk,
Have spread through all the forest near.
You hear the saw from dawn to dark,
Shi and *shi*, *shi* and *shi*.
Their home is in the mountains where
The day begins, beyond the sea.

In couples, one who stands upright,
The other facing, on his knees.
The kneeling man is bent and white,
The one who stands is the younger one.
What powerful arms among the trees
Move up and down, up and down!

Only the robin watches them,
Now from a branch, now from the ground.
It hops and flies from stone to stem
And twirls and flutters, tree to tree,
And sends its sweet refrain around
Between the sounds of *shi* and *shi*.

The Saint required a plumb-straight line
To mark his block of cypress wood.
Now Mary, suckling her Son,
Was in the house beside the fire,
But there at hand the robin stood.
Saint Joseph called to it: "Come here."

He dipped his sponge in dye, and red
He stained his string with sinopite.
"This end, take in your beak," he said.
"Stand here and hold it carefully."
Mary in her loved retreat
Missed the sound of *shi* and *shi*.

Now silent, he unwound the twine
From off its reel, along the beam,
And drew it back, stretched taut and fine,
Ready to rebound upon...
But through the air an "Ave" came:
There was Mary with her Son.

The bird flashed round, and all askew
The red string slipped and marked the beam.
The Saint snatched up his sponge and threw...
And stained its feathers. So we see
Why now the redbreast is its name.
And when it hears the *shi* and *shi*

It still will come between the boughs
To watch and flutter, watch and sing;
And though it will not come so close,
For it is wiser now than then,
Its song consoles their wandering,
Poor exiled tribe, the foreign men.

VII *Later Poems from*
THE SPACE BETWEEN

A Monochrome Photograph

As flowers set fruit, as liquids vaporise,
Colour has turned to light,
Or as our world's particularities
In some imagined heaven might –
All colours there dissolved in white.

So here on the low and rising slopes of hills
In groups and scattered places
Set at their beautiful chance intervals
The trees shine white on darker spaces,
Taking the transverse light on their faces.

All the calm scene is filled with mystery,
By what outlandish moon? –
Colour to light, earth changed to poetry.
Yet he said, "Autumn, evening sun,"
Showing his prints to us one by one,

And named the hills; and we saw how he had seen it,
A landscape strewn with fire;
How taking light he had quenched that colour in it
To make a world so strange and clear
Only in dreams could one enter there.

Imagined Flowers

Flowers of extraordinary beauty –
As, rare in woods, the green
And white helleborine;
Luminous by washed walls the fuchsia
With pendant lamps like fruits of summer –
Visit my idle sight
Fallow by day or night,
As tunes beset and haunt the dreamer.

Deep as a well the air is round them –
Stone that casts vivid shade,
Light filtered to a glade
Or trees' or evening's darkness on them.
Or their own leaves lap cool and sallow
To island them in space –
As in a foreign face
The eyes shine from a deeper hollow.

Seen or imagined out of season
This beauty seems to stand
With meaning in its hand,
Yet will not answer rhyme or reason:
Beauty that obviates expression,
Lustre of earth that is
Not for our purposes
And least of all things courts our passion.

Pain has its Innocence

Pain has its innocence: extremity
Of sorrow lends its own pure quality.
Freak tides that drown the soul awhile confer
A lustre that is theirs and not of her.
The ruined lands lie bare when deep floods fall;
Awhile now, crystal water covers all.

On the River with Friends

1

It was green on the river
And a settled summer day
Serene as though for ever.

Now the willows lay
Their leaves along the stream
And here a finger may

Be trailed of one of them
And here may plunge a wrist;
And now their shade and gleam

In low sun fall to east,
Across the flow to where
We tie the boat and rest.

2

Hard to catch that blue
Lace-winged pleasure, light,
Quiet, half attended to.

For talk unfocused sight,
Yet presences confused
And drift of dark and bright

Swayed the words we used:
Green forms, and the constant sway
Whether we stayed or cruised

Of water; sense of the day
And summer, not two but one,
And still, not flowing away.

3

Casual was all we said
But the words came to our ears
From far accompanied.

Friends of thirty years,
There is no urgency
In talk as long as ours,

But summer's eternity
And a fair day's careless wonder
Of calm, illusory

Yet true, as the river under
Its willows borne abides.
Now the spell may break in thunder.

An Ordinary Autumn

Leaves dying and the light of autumn speak of death
And poetry. The light's hallucinatory calm
Though known for fragile seems eternal over earth;
And the leaves, as beloved and numberless as words,
Emptied of function, look towards their dying storm.

And yet it is an ordinary autumn, with the birds
Intent on the last pears fallen, and through holes in the net
Of summer more naked in their coming and going,
And the leaves' selves not miraculously bright
As some years, fallen to ashy fairness, or still showing

Their dark green, like experience worn. And still the light
Oblique and tempered is as wonderful as gold,
And the gold brush-strokes of the leaves of Solomon-seal
Sign the garden; all is common; I being old
(And that is common too) this year more dearly feel
The metaphor of autumn painted on the world.

In a Foreign Land

Dark is to me this forested country.
Sweet rustling words are hard to follow
And roots of nameless trees along the heart lie shallow.

But water is one the whole world over.
Not strange is light on any inland river
Nor strange, in the wide famous estuary for ever

The enormous tide, just as in any other,
On its open palm, in its candid power
Lifting the water-weed, the cradle leaf and flower.

The Sandy Yard

One day at noon I crossed
A sandy yard planted with citrus trees
Behind a small hotel. I walked slowly in the sun
With feet in the hot sand which the leaf-cutting ants
Crossed too, under their little sails of green, filing
Intent; and I thought, this
I will keep, I will register with time: I am here;
And always, shall have been here – that is the wonder –
Never, now, not have been here; for now I am here,
Crossing the sandy yard
Between the citrus trees, behind the small hotel.

The Expatriate Girl

From our land of spring
And autumn and cold seas and long
Shadows journeying
She has built her house among

The sharp simplicities:
The mountains and the royal sea,
The noonday shadowless trees,
And poverty, and gaiety.

Now she lays her head
On the volcanic beaches and
Her northern hair is spread
On their jet and crystal sand.

Power Cut

Without a word the light dropped and the radio voice
Fell sheer to silence. So by fire's and torch's light
And curtains opened on unnatural natural night
Clouded and starry – on a top shelf, another year's
Dusty candle I have found and lit; and there
It burns (I wish, for ever) making within its range
An unassertive harmony, yet slightly strange,
Subtle and mild and strange, with the dark and the fire.
No light to read by nor extrinsic voice, we can
Talk, or dream in silence like the fire, like the flowers
In the candle's web; like the very old. I think of powers
Failing, my generation ageing, dying, gone;
And think those happy who have candle-light and coals
To modify and charm the dark when the power fails.

African Violets

What is it that draws eyes so in these flowers'
Intensity of colour? Is it the blackness
Implicit there? As violet sleeps in the darkness
Of darkest human skin, so black in these.

Who mixed this pigment surely had in mind
Crowns for dark vivid children playing on mountains
Or wooded shores where Afric's sunny fountains
(Once we sang rapt) roll down their golden sand.

But what is it draws eyes as if to doors
Swung wide on night? What is it that releases
Imagination so to calms and spaces
Through such small doors as the dark that sleeps in the flowers?

And why should it speak of anything but itself,
This little plant merely present, signally present
As beauty is, under the fluorescent
Light or in daylight on a basement shelf?

182

Winter Song

Between two ice ages
Before the shortest day,
Walking in the mild air
And on the yielding clay

And on the grassy tussocks
That fill their rifts and caves
As dark and bright as violet beds
With sodden drifted leaves,

Walking in the green winter
That has drunk the snow
We talk as sea-borne strangers would
When travelling was slow.
Spring is in doubt, a death ahead,
Summer, a life ago.

Alloway's Guides

He closed his book and told this tale to me,
I tell again for what I found it worth:
In love with space, in love with stringency
Alloway journeyed to the ends of the earth.

In the bloom of empire and exploration
He climbed unclimbed mountains and traversed ranges
Doubtfully mapped, and he crossed the central Asian
Desert, in love with extremity and strangeness.

There travelling with camels by night in the hot season
With three men (guides and servant) he watched the guides
Steer by the stars with infallible precision
Over a thousand miles immune to roads.

And once there trudging through gravelly sand beside
The camels, through days without landmarks like the plain,
He saw a man sprint ahead – the younger guide –
Grow small and vanish – and asked where he had gone.

"His home is here. No doubt he has gone home."
So they caught up with him by the poor tents,
Four in number, pitched by a trickle of stream
In the pure unkindness of soil and elements

At the ends of the earth; and he for his few pence,
The blithe serene young man, came on with them.
Alloway thought of the ranges of experience,
And envied him, and fell to dreams of home.

Tropical Gardens

I remember a courtyard set with frangipani trees
Like an orchard, apple-tree tall. Flowers – sweetly and dryly
      scented
Like no other, white, the corolla deeply indented –
Even fallen, lie whole on the grass. Dear life that has flowers like
      these.

Again in a paradisal garden that sloped to a river
I saw those trees among many – flamboyant, Spanish pride...
On the scarlet tree, in its feathered green, where the flowers had
      died
The few left shone the more, the sooty pods hung over.

These in the fresh warm garden that fell to the river-side
I remember again, and the river, the Amazon that passes
Floating the water hyacinth, gentling the grasses.
Oh, wide, yet for wooded islands you could not tell how wide.

They sieved its power as merciful cloud makes down the sun's,
Till strained to simple beauty, nothing but beauty, fit
For shallow visitant eyes, as sometimes, sometimes not,
Fate scales to our tourist dreams its too-great Amazons.

But wide, wide enough, at the foot of the cared-for flowering-
Tree-burnished garden, this great one shone in the unvaried
Sunrise, and easily with night and daylight carried
Its fame and fable by, with its small boats, unhurrying.

The Geese on the Park Water

1

The Canada geese
Pose in the light and dark of ripples,
And in and out of narrow shadows
Pose, compose, improvising
Their endless eloquent line.

And elongated, dissolved by ripples,
Cast by the trees, tree-casts, the shadows
Are only material for the posing,
Are driftwood salvaged for the composing,
The endless flow-away improvising
Of the Canada geese.

2

Like the arts that exist in time
Alone or essentially –
Acting, dancing, even
Music and poetry –
The lives of men and of birds,
The line their living scores
Upon time, the notes or words
Are as if performed. But for whom?

For us the dancing; the elegant
Water-birds if they pose
These do not pose for us
Though their existence flows
Away in forms that to us
Are grace, grace flowing out
Like water wasted in drought
Constantly into unbeing.

Time is a sluice set open
And through it, we mourn, too fast
All beauty shown or spoken,
Apprehended, runs to the past.
Yet what quells my mind the most
Is not the loved and known

But the unregarded un-
Apprehended constantly flowing,

Unless there is God, to waste;
As, when the gates close, unseen,
Unknown (as we think of knowing)
The Canada geese on the lake
Will transpose from now to the past
(For now, while we say it, is past)
Will compose for time and death
(For time is promised to death)

Their endless eloquent line.

Figures in a Photograph

A second time pregnant, so knowing that country, she
Who at any age may have loved to dream dreamlessly
On sea beaches now especially
Dreams, though with eyes for the child, with words for the other,
The older woman, mother-in-law or mother,
Who walks with her by the ritual wave of the sea.

The child from swinging on the hand of either
Has darted on through the shine from sand and water.
This is the one who beat the pathways with her
Of a new-found world. "She has been there before"
The older woman thinks, strolling the shore
Beside her dreaming daughter-in-law or daughter.

They are mid-distant, giving the scene its scale.
Yet their humanity has changed the fall
Of light through clouds to bright, theatric, frail –
Frail as their moment's attention that sees, half sees
The wave and the burnished sand, and the headland's wall
As far again, and the green of its evergreen trees.

The Unused Morning

On a long column scarcely fluted
The early daylight lifts its day's hours,
And in our garden the southern hemisphere's
Lilies on their long columns raise
Through individual silences,
Beyond the curtain, spires of fine-drawn flowers

Like southern stars, like and unlike
Our own lilies, our imprinted constellations.
But I, how long now have I been awake
Or in and out of sleep, a seagull skimming
Its lifted waves; a loafer dreaming
In doorways of a constant summer region?

In summer or a summer land,
Idling from in to out-of-doors, returning,
Is a light drifting between open rooms.
All thresholds dissipate; the dust enters and
The warm air like a house-dog goes and comes –
As we through sleep in the unused morning.

Two Visits to a Hillside

The children from overseas are on the chalk hill
Picking the almost stemless flowers: small
Among the whitening flints gentian, hawkweed
And flowers too many and obscure to tell.
The little girl says, "Girls pick flowers to smell them,
Boys pick them to mash them." But if we say
We like the flowers, without a word they lay
Each at our feet a doll's-house-sized bouquet,
Smile and are gone for other flowers to swell them.

And later, lower down, where stones out-star
All gold and blood-drop flowers – treating rough ground
And thorned shrubs carefully, prospecting there
Alone and self-contained, the boy has found

An island continent of blackberries,
Australia of strange fruits, and brings to us
A palmful of specimens; and we say yes,
Eat some and keep us some; and so he does,
So both do, dark on the white galaxies.

That was late summer; now the year is failing.
The children have gone home across the ocean.
Here are a few blackberries, soggy in the trailing
Vague sweet autumn, and brown spikelets of gentian.
And still the slope with its stone immortelles
Is dyed with dark and small intensities
Where the children played (as a light or window is
Found printed under eyelids when they close);
Still printed with his bearing, with her songbird calls.

The Cross-Country Journey

Seen by the passenger, the further the range
The slowlier it will change (yet it will change)
But what is near beyond the window-ledges,
Half seen, is gone: the cattle by the hedges,
The section of canal, the beaten lanes,
The children in their faithful love of trains
Waving from fences, hanging over bridges.

So we in our slow lives – for they seem slow,
Though what can we compare with all we know? –
Journeying cross-country watch the loved and near
Run by, till dazzled we rest eyes on the far,
On the abstract hills, on the unresponding
Beauty of earth, or the sun let down to a landing
Or entering rooms where the drifts of memory are.

The foreground flashes on – there by the willows
They are bathing now, as we were in the shallows
Of middle age lately or long ago –
While still the hills maintain the journey slow,
Accompanying us as after dark the moon might,
As now the sun... yet the slant itself of the sunlight
Assents to change, with all the world we know.

To an Infant Grandchild

Dear Katherine, your future
Can never meet my past.
So short our common frontier,
Our hinterlands so vast.

Yet at the customs post
Light airs pass freely over
And all we need to know
We know of one another.

Though day will wake your country
As dark flows over mine
Your outback sleeps in shadow now.
Your smile is cloudless dawn.

Soloists

1

The awaited moment, the ballerina parts
The chorus and her solo dancing starts.
She is modest and small like the rest. Her rarity
Is in lightness and clarity.

With a silver hammer she strikes each note
Once and singly. Then is carried apart
Or absorbed into the choral dance again.
Her friends take her in.

Again at an awaited moment the solo
Piano's voice will enter the concerto.
In the heart of a forest's multiple murmuring
It rises like a spring,

And the orchestra parts its complexity
To let its tutelary spirit free.
And rests from sound. The cadenza takes its way
Straying, but cannot stray

Out of perfection. And always – far though it runs,
By single notes like the dancer – as it returns
The orchestra will stretch out hands again,
Take its hand, and whirl it in.

2

Beyond those two another comes to mind:
A child who is in and out, away, around,
Who speaks to the gathered elders and returns
To his own place and concerns.

A child so young can have charm like genius –
For whether that charm remains with him or goes
Now he draws eyes as surely as a rose
Or as the dancer does,

And speaks to ears' enchantment like that sprite
The pianist called from the forest to run in the light,
And like these in their seeming waywardness, will be gone,
No telling when to return.

Under obedience, in pure artistry
Enclosed, they mime his spontaneity –
Nature's – however higher they may coil than he
Where the vine of being winds on its tree.

Strollers in a Park

1

One thing was new in the much visited park,
In the cooling air, day turning early towards dark,
On the stone bridge over the man-made width of the lake.

They were grazing sheep in the park; it was this was unwonted.
Thirty...a hundred...two hundred say, he counted
And reckoned, crossing the bridge unattended,

Jostling, accommodating, as the sand
Streams in an hour-glass, from the green broads beyond
To out-fan again over the near-side ground.

"I have never seen so many pressing through
Field gates or straying on fells," she said; "it is true
Always, lacing the old we meet the new."

They took the bridge after the last stragglers
Had crossed and the lame ones and the unambitious
Were cropping the sweet home grass among the others

In patriarchal calm spread far and wide
Between the great façade and the waterside,
Now nonchalant and satisfied.

2

The lake draws in for the bridge, and on both sides
Spreads (as the sheep flock narrowed and now spreads)
As far each way as beauty alone decides.

Below the bridge, on every shelf of its piers
Domestic pigeons settle and converse,
Whose murmuring cannot but seem love's to us.

The strollers paused in mute community
By one then the other parapet. Each way
Water and land had been changed to please the eye,

Yet seemed – because the artist had judged well
And because light is powerful over all –
Under the clouded sun seemed natural.

And we are nature's, and our seeing is
A part, she thought, also a part of this.
The silver stretches were infinities.

"We have come here many times; we shall not come
As many more." "But some," he said; "but some."
They watched through glasses before turning home

Mallard and coot on the darker water, made
So dark by the further trees' shelter and shade.
"And we have seen today's new thing," she said.

Autumn Song

Now bell-shaped pears are hung
From every least twig's end
Where the pear-tree never pruned
Arches down symmetrically:
Cavernous, but how leafy;
A fountain, yet so heavy
That the water-drops in wind
Hardly swerve, nor the dense bells are swung

Ever enough to ring.
And flowers of summer, one
Beyond another following
Through gardens and through time, now these
That were ranged in the border
As hills are in their order
Dissolve, and birds speak of unease
In drifts and feints of flight and moody loitering.

Summer was not for long,
Autumn our longest season.
The rim of winter's shadow lies on
Autumn now, strange, not ungentle, only strong.

Judgement Day

If it should come to pass, and we found ourselves
Helplessly truthful – like someone in deep shock
Giving his first statement to the police
After the fatal accident: "I swerved."
"I took my eyes off him." "I thought I had time." –

Or someone before doctors, describing his pains
With his best candour and his anxious eyes,
Undressing as instructed like a child
And after the examination going
Where he is told – if it should come to this

And we before authority should be bound
To tell the most complex truth in the simplest words
(Which the bench should have the skill to understand)
Then surely, after sentence, helplessly
Truthful, without pretence or anxiety,
We would take whatever fate, how nearly happily.

Workers in Metal

Working surely overtime, the scaffolders
Against the evening sky of early winter
With their skill's panache and the dissonant music of metal
Between tall houses raised their handsome structure,
And now itself it has taken on the tone
Of age, because the builders not the next
Nor any day the winter through returned.

Well, we are in their hands who are at home
With metal, whether it may be the bold
Against the sky night-faring scaffolders;
Or dreamers of machines for peace or war;
Or those who in the chairman's room
Dispose the imaginary gold.

A Photograph from Abroad

The dark child in her darker than sky-blue dress,
Tall, pliant, pretty, seven or eight years old –
Posed for her photograph to bend and hold
One of the stems (as obediently she does)
Of the plant that patterns the verandah's view –
The child on the lacy verandah and the tropical
Pennon-leaved shrub straying over sky and all,
They make a design that might be a poem too.

And so I wrote to her mother. What, though, seeing
That in the way of mysterious light expression
Of a small beauty, all is done, what are words to
Express or be? What is the poem to do?
Nothing to do but follow its vocation.
Nothing to be but tribute to what is in being.

The Pensioner

At the time of morning when the recesses
In bedroom walls stand forward like tall ghosts,
And as curtains thin, the fine wings of the swarms
That flecked the dark catch a softer and generalised light,
And furniture takes up its being and weight,
And it is our world again whose nightly dissolved
White foam is again overriding the dark of its sea:

At such a time of day in early or late
Winter the pensioner, old man or woman
Cast up on morning, may forebode the cold,
And foresee beyond the eastward curtains, beyond
The shrubs and roof-tops, those now leafless trees,
Those shapes of poplars whose beauty even more
Than on the sky is imprinted on his days.

And he may think the sky will be beautiful
As well, with sunrise fantasies – or plain,
Neutral or rainy, no matter; the birds may at
The drawing of curtains explode, though softly, away
From their bare twigs or chosen evergreens,
But he will have seen them, starlings, chaffinches,
Perhaps a thrush; domestic as their names.

And he may foretell going down through the muted cold
Of the house, filling the kettle, making tea,
And feel the deed adventurous, something done
A first or last time (as fragility
And strangeness cast their colours); and foretaste
The warmth of the tea; and may go to meet the familiar,
Adhering to it, knowing beyond thought it is not for ever.

The Young Couple

So this young couple came to see me – why
I have forgotten, and what their names might be.
I did not know them, but as if long known
I more than liked, I loved them. We sat down
Awhile. Perhaps they had come with some idea
Of buying the house, for we wandered here and there.
She said, "The spare-room?" "At the turn of the stair."
She came back saying, "I cannot find a door."
I went with her; there was no room at all
At the turn of the stair. There was a papered wall
And a window on the garden, as before
The house was altered, long before our time.
So then I understood. I said, "My dear,
We are figures in a dream." I said to them
"Perhaps it is your dream," for pity's sake,
"And you will wake." I thought they would not wake.
I kissed their fading lips that never spoke
Again, who had been my friends. And so I woke.

Reflection in a Café

There is a time of life, or so it seems,
When the innocence of young children widens out
To enclose their parents in its globe of light.

The little red-haired girl with chestnut eyes
Moved in the café between her darker mother's
Care, and her chestnut-eyed and -bearded father's.

And they were happy: it was no more than that.
She was subdued, then lively; yet sedate.
Her father fed to her chips from his plate.

In the Basement Room

In the window of the room, in our cave's adit,
Between falls of the vine and the lichen-green acrylic,
We keep each year a vase of that year's papery
Seeds, the Americans with more simplicity
Call Silver Dollars, we
As if from long experience call Honesty.

Shadowy, spotted, nacreous, not silver, less than white...
Loved by the light: only for them the last of light
Enters the basement room, slipped through the pavement's bars,
By the streaked and ferny area wall, through the window glass
To the seeds in their cold vase –
Pervious or light-reflecting, never not luminous.

A million years ago we brought the flawed and pearled
Gift of our honesty to the thousand million of our world's
By mind neglected garden: we brought our consciousness,
Such as it is; if silver, tarnished; fatal – none the less
No yard of earth but has
Been dwelt upon by us, been loved by some of us.

If I held any creed, at this time I would pray
To whatever light might mean in my faith's imagery:
"Do not forsake us now. Such as we are, we are
– Translucent or reflecting – your best lovers here;
We only, apt for incandescence when you come
To your neglected garden, to your basement room."

A Beach in the Antilles

In the late afternoon the sun in fast decline
Still struck from the sands of ash their pewter shine.
The light-boned children still played on the water-line.

Three women all the day had watched or swum,
And talked, and served the meal when it was time.
In the late afternoon there fell on them,

Over and round them, a slow snow of white
Flowers, flowers fallen not blown, in light
Showers or singly from the moderate height

Of the wooded cliff. None of us knew the name
Of the flowers nor knew, as slowly we noticed them,
From which tall tree, sprawled up the cliff, they came;

But they came to rest, a few at first on the sand
As if they had grown there, then over the strewn ground
On a cast shoe, in a drained cup, on a hand,

On a net or a shell: trumpet flowers, candle white.
And if they had been butterflies, as by their flight
They almost seemed, they could give no more delight,

Signing the day's perfection so, at the fall of night.

The Question

This world whose variegated skin is channelled
By the haphazard wasp, by larvae tunnelled,
Seems a fruit ripening to windfall – though meanwhile
Mottled and sunned with marks as beautiful
As birds' elaborate wings, or eggs that nature
Patterns or children decorate for Easter.

But on what tree does this fruit hang heavily?
And in what garden or orchard grows that tree?
What nest of gardens in suburbs of what city
Or orchard belt in lowlands of what country?
Mapped on what world, world turning in what air?
Where thought refuses, ignorance loiters there.

The Dead

The dead are music, the dead are poetry.
The hero dead is a ballad, the child dead is a song,
A rounded water-drop, seamless, a few lines long,
And the first and the last lines are the same

So that it can be sung on and on.
The living are told in verbs, the dead is a noun alone.
The living are prose, and with prose what varied things can be
    done!
But the dead is a poem: the poem is solely a name.

Unstrained

These flowers' beauties were unstrained,
Their stillness, pausing of the wind,
Before my coming laid its human
Abstract intensity upon them
And made a difference I did not intend.

Young children's ways come near their way –
Who pick and drop them easily
Or give (not knowing live from dead)
For gift a clutched and stemless head.
"Pretty", not "beautiful", young children say.

"Pretty" is lighter than a feather
And moves through flowers like natural weather.
These flowers of phlox in their rosy range
Being called pretty does not change.
But "beautiful" is heavier altogether,

And lays on lives that should be free
Our love charged with mortality.
The air is stilled in expectation.
Each bridal flower waits at its station...
And yet they are not waiting, nor know of ecstasy.

The Expected Storm

Not overnight, but the thunder came
In the morning, when the absolute rain hung straight
On the lead of its own weight.

Lightning, no more than the blink of a lid,
Was it – or not? And few but far asunder
The seconds passed, till thunder

Said "Aye" – thunder with its lovely offshoots, stray
Afterthoughts of its dying away, renewals of sound
Like music the composer cannot bear to end.

And the Thames Valley drank its rightful rain
As if it would never stop; as eventually one
Deprived of sleep drinks his due of it on and on.

The Evening Garden

Not dark nor light but clear,
But lucid with no source of light,
But breathing with no flow of air
The garden journeys into night.

Late gangling flowers lean –
Anemones, tobacco flowers –
Over the gravel, over the brown
And silken leaves that mulch the grass.

More than I did, I now
Leave in this lighted room undrawn
The curtains. More than it used to do
The garden presses on the pane,

Or seems it does, in this
One hour when all is seeming, when
It wars with shadowy lights in the glass,
And losing, is most potent then –

Only in this one hour,
Tidal, returns – day's utmost edge –
Pressing with eyes of question or power,
Gold wild-cat eyes on the window-ledge.

Walled plot of fruit-trees, flowers,
What strength it wields, how hard it bears!
Why should it not bear hard? It has
Behind it all the universe.

The lighted room is small.
Now we exist; and now we fashion
A garden and a girdling wall,
Our salient into wild creation.

The Space Between

From this high window best, you see the briar rose
In its short flowering – how the yellow one has spread
Rangy above the white on the deep-sea garden bed;
As clouds lie over clouds in archipelagos,
But small as petals on the grass, under the wing
Of the soaring plane. And are they clouds or can they be,
Those deepest down, foam flecks or mountain waves of sea?
Our eyes are dazed by nature's see-through curtaining,

Layer upon layer stretched, woven to all degrees
Of part-transparency: the rose, knotted like lace
To a star pattern, thins between to stellar space.
Though eyes before they learn level the galaxies,
It is not the flowers' selves only, webbed in their skies of green,
It is depth they grant to sight; it is the space between.

VIII
From LISTENING TO COLLARED DOVES

The Scent

She had forgotten, talking, in her hand
Were roses. Otherwise how could it be
Their scent had come upon her unawares
And seemed a stray from thought or memory,
A shoot or spring of deepest clear content
Breaking out from the dark ground of the mind,
Before she understood the scent was theirs,
Before she recognised it as a scent?
As happiness can meet one waked from sleep
And not at first bring back to mind its cause
And close its wings of light upon its small
And mortal bones and take its given shape,
So that bliss hung, before it claimed it was
Her roses' scent, or had a name at all.

The Red Chrysanthemum

This small and many flowered chrysanthemum
Of the darkest red that still can be called bright,
Compliant to cutting, in evening light, lamp light
Most glows, declares itself, seems most to come
Into its own. We warm hands at radiance
That is neither weak nor strong but set between
Where comfort is, where in tumult of dark green
Branching and leaves, a clement fire haunts.

This world is partly tuned to intercourse
With us – part not, but where it is, how well! –
As when, on hard lives in a backward land,
On the rice in the pot, on the earth of familiar floors,
On the path to water, the kindness of beauty will fall;
At times there too close wings and come to hand.

Images of Age

The sluggish changes that are not seen till done,
The palace revolutions out of the blue,
When they come true seem long to have been true.
I have heard, where the Negro meets the Amazon

And black transparent and white waters join
(The white opaque with silt, emulsified)
A stretch, unmixed, the two flow side by side
Till the white overwhelms. Age must come on,

When sleep invading blood in the veins moves.
Then dreams are narrow runnels under moss,
Almost, barely, the moor grass meets across –
Blue of the sky on its strawy lacing leaves.

The Locust Trees

Especially now when the low sun
Is early lost behind invisible mist
Or sunk beyond the roof-tops north of west,
And in that quarter all the sky is one
White incandescence, shading towards pale flame
Only at the earth's rim,

Especially now the trees, not native
Here, garden trees, put their foreign aspect on;
And most they do since the massive beech has gone –
By which their group or little landscaped grove
Is thinned to a flying strangeness affined to air,
And the trees show their stature more:

The locust trees, that human might
Tell out their difference by some different grace,
As the shape of eyes can bemuse in an English face.
Being trees, how do they tell it? By sparse and light
High branching, as if they had vied for the sun
In natural forests; leaves of rain

In the air, not falling; by their response
To wind, fluid as water's; but the most
As now, when laid upon the Atlantic west
In the evening lull of wind, and still this once,
Black wording on such white, how long ago they seem
Printed, how far away, by whom?

The Confidence

So she told her Greek story
Facing the daylight window,
Her gull-grey eyes opaque
And swept of shadow:
Monstrous, grievous, heroic,
Like something legendary
Yet not to be re-told
Till the end of the world.

Massive as kings' tombs,
Secret as graves grassed over,
Larger than life though life
Is large, this grief.
Friend, brave enough, not braver
But equal to what comes,
The words that would be tender
Are lost in wonder.

Domestic

The house has come to life with the first fire of autumn.
The coal burns sluggishly, but the seed of fire has entered.
The house will bear the winter.

Bereaved the wild-haired garden leans towards the past.
Gales rough its white and purple weeds that mourn for summer.
The house fore-dreams the winter.

Used carelessly in the good days, a shed or shelter;
A half-way house, indoors to out, in rootless autumn
(Blown leaves distract its flooring) –

Now to be cosseted, now valued, impregnated
With dark and cold, with warmth, warm voices, curtains drawn,
It comes into its own.

Night Scene from Indoors

Twelve is still evening: friends are talking late.
The small hours, two or three, are true midnight.
And yet obliquely across the lane a light
Shines, forgotten by charmed talkers, on.
Pure night: no least intelligence of dawn.

Racemes of the laburnum still hang down,
Flowers turned to seed-pods, gold to green to brown.
There was a day between green and brown, they shone
As if in a second flowering. For certain trees
This was a miracle spring, and among them these.

They are heavy now in August with fruit of their kind.
The stems sway, hung with baubles, offerings. Wind
Lights them as the street-lamp shines from behind
With that late house-lamp. They catch a leaf in their beam,
Or tassel of tinsel, candles lit among them:

A Christmas tree lit for a festival
At a day's mid-winter. It seemed a natural
Earth-sized enchantment; though one star proved it small,
Sighted far, cold, beyond thought. Tinsel, oh true,
Is tinsel. Yet it is known by radiance too.

Listening to Collared Doves

I am homesick now for middle age, as then
For youth. For youth is our home-land: we were born
And lived there long, though afterwards moved on
From state to state, too slowly acclimatising
Perhaps and never fluent, through the surprising
Countries, in any languages but one.

This mourning now for middle age, no more
For youth, confirms me old as not before.
Age rounds the world, they say, to childhood's far
Archaic shores; it may be so at last.
But what now (strength apart) I miss the most
Is time unseen like air, since everywhere.

And yet, when in the months and in the skies
That were the cuckoos', and in the nearer trees
That were the deep-voiced wood-pigeons', it is
Instead now the collared doves that call and call
(Their three flat notes growing traditional),
I think we live long enough, listening to these.

I draw my line out from their simple curve
And say, our natural span may be enough;
And think of one I knew and her long life;
And how the climate changed and how the sign-
Posts changed, defaced, from her Victorian
Childhood and youth, through our century of grief;

And how she adapted as she could, not one
By nature adaptable, bred puritan
(Though quick to be pleased and having still her own
Lightness of heart). She died twenty years ago,
Aged, of life – it seems, all she could do
Having done, all the change that she could know having known.

Bright Margins

I thought of decoration, such as once was done
To frame a manuscript – how the finished work is one,
Cornflowers and gold are one with the marmoreal
Script, with the firm and sounding Latin words as well
And the meaning of the words – no meaning but a bell

Whose overtones dissolve its note that would be clear;
And thought again – in the wide borders of the year
Walking by blue and golden flowers and like the moon
Self-shadowed white, short-lived in autumn garden beds
That are bright margins too – how they seem the silk of thread,
Not woven in the cloth, embroideries, not the words
Nor the meaning of the words; and still the work is one.

A Picnic Place

I am diffident to take into my thought
Out of their separate cot,
Afraid to overlie
And stifle such small pleasures come to light
As these first dwarfed and crumpled flowers of white
Dead-nettle in their leaves of purplish dye

In the backward country spring, in the always
Rough look of roadside grass,
Anarchic, unaligned,
In hemlock, common nettles – nothing over
A foot high under the north-western wind
Between the farm track and the swollen river.

In gardens of the suburbs spring comes early –
Daffodils over nearly,
Pansies, even tulips. Trees
That have forgotten their ancestral home
Flower in angelic order. We have come
To different wintrier realities.

No birds down-stream. There was a light far on
I thought to be a swan,
But that proved as it twirled
To be some floundering casing or carton,
Some reject of the inorganic world
Our river took for swan and would not drown.

And yet it never flowed so fast nor fuller
Nor was so bronze in colour
Nor held in fine suspension
So much of earth. If there are fish, the kingfisher
No more than we, you said, sees them down there.
No moorhen would put out on this churned ocean.

Out of the wind in the car we drink our coffee,
And in the always scruffy
Wayside grass that use and wont
Make beautiful, I see the white-flowered nettle,
A little crumpled, leafed and stemmed in purple.
Nothing here need be perfect to enchant.

Michaelmas Evenings

1

Dark rainy day,
And night delivers itself early.
Has it ever been away?

Yet fiery, unnaturally
Brilliant, enlarged the berries; grass
Shines after rain more clearly

Illuminating these
Margins of night – though twilight flowers
Most briefly at Michaelmas.

Amethyst daisies, asters, bluer than violet:
Better than words embroidery silks might imitate
Colour and shape, but not the lightness of their state,

Riding at anchor in the uninsistent air;
Dégagé as those saints that in church windows wear
Casual bright translucence. How can anywhere

Such lightness, such intensity so co-exist?
By the yellow leaves of the vine, now in the almost last
Of visibility, such blue and amethyst?

First and Late Snow

The snow holds, on the grass and leaves
Of evergreens and earthen ground.
The rose denies it, tree that loves
Translucency and will suspend
Its diamonds long after rain –
The small twigs lacing chain with chain,
Light caught in weightless lightness. So
It makes a dew of snow, denying snow,

And has its way. The opaque will crumble.
Snow was a feint, the rain takes over.
And yet this drenched vernal autumnal
Winter, this mere default of summer
Has said at last its ritual word.
Perhaps enough... How, while it stayed
The snow defined the branches' slanting,
How it unloosed its flakes! Nothing was wanting.

Seeing the Baby

Far down he seems to sleep on the ground of a pool
Trees overcast or a deep well.
Yet the water is clear; the shadow-colour thrown
On the white sheet is all his own,
The tender sallow that is warm as cool.

You lend me your child, so nearly new, to see.
If I should touch him it would be
A different thing, but the long shaft of sight
Isolates as a field-glass might,
And the deep walls of the cradle simplify.

He could not be smaller and still human. Flowers
Encapsulate a world for us.
Jewels pack large in small, of beauty, cost,
Strangeness. Of all on earth, he most
Most stores in little substance: human, ours.

At the Gate of the Junior School

Here is the gate with the young parents waiting there –
Some of them beautiful but not, as once they were,
As flowers are beautiful, no longer in that way.
Their used and hardy beauties are in fruit today.

Life for its reasons has them in its exigent employ –
Talking their in-group talk, watching for girl or boy.
And the children come, flickering like flames over cindery ground.
Each, they reclaim their own. Life has them in its hand.

The Long Grass

Our love was deep in the long grass
As clover flowers – not deeper was.
Not deeper are the ocean beds.
It was all that earth needs.

IX   *Later Uncollected Poems*

The Hands of the Blind

As we are conscious of the hands of the blind
So learned with a different lore from ours,
Seeing the fingers like movements of a mind –
Slightly recurved, the distal phalanges
With their silk touch reading the universe;

Or as we may surprise on a blind face
The transit of a smile, like that on a young
Baby's alone, private, protectionless,
And sense another world, a silver one,
A moon before our landings on the moon;

And may in our complementary blindness grope
To touch pure nescience of sight, that bears
Gifts such as only choose its mode and scope –
In the fenced garden its particular flowers –
So I believe, of worlds further from ours,

To minds, not eyes, born dark, there must open vistas,
Lights burn in savage hearts. In tropical
Forests strange flowers, beaked heliconias
Amaze; on utmost snow sky colours fall –
Blindnesses, visions, being the gifts of us all.

A Portrait of a Boy

He frowns a little, facing the light.
The large leaves' shadows blot and camouflage
Him, laurel-shaped leaves and broad wings of poinsettia.

He has folded his arms, being eleven,
A proud age, and looks forward wholly directly
Out of the shadows, though he frowns a little

As if the light and the open prospect
Were adulthood, and he considering it
With all his attention, mustering all he can

Out of his leaf-pied childhood; and further
As if he were Man emergent from the forest
Of animal nature, Adam confronting his fate –

Knowledge, the shelterless light-washed spaces
Spread for him on and on – and bringing to bear
Consciousness: his integrity, all that he has.

The Fish in the Evenlode

That there is so much more than this
I know; and yet there is
That dark and stubborn fish that stays
Below the stream's engaging surface ways
And might be dozing in a sluggish dream
Yet keeps its place against the stream, headed upstream.

Like hair alive in water, here gilded on green
The long combed weeds flow and within
The shiftings of their flow the fish is seen, unseen.

And here in summer
White flowers of crowfoot will star over
The penetrable dusk of the small river,
Fairer than if some artist in Japan
Had touched them in faultlessly one by one
For nothing but delight, on his dark folding screen.

And still, moving nor moved, the fish lies low.
Its strength is equal to the water's flow.
Its name I surely know –
Self-will, the body's will, older than birth,
The creature's will (unwilled) to be and thrive on earth.

Solomon's Seal

I have never looked at the root, not seen that five
Or six-pointed star, the flower-books differ on,
The seal itself, emblem of Solomon.
Only the scalloped bells hung from their curve
Touch me with silence of their green-fringed white,
As guessed on grassy mountains sheep-bells might.

And the bowed stems themselves know endlessly
How best to please; curving above their bells,
It may be with a wave's or waterfall's
Simplicity of line, pure symmetry,
Or ·deviant to some perfect abstruse
Degree, they answer to what need in us?

Outdoors they wear a rushing look. Past rain
Still rides their leaves in globes like mercury.
Arranged indoors they are form, they are statuary.
But I would choose to be the objective, plain
Flower draughtsman I have envied, or some bold
Searcher for truth through the worm-conditioned mould
Who finds on roots the star-shaped seal like gold.

Green in January

Though it was not the true green, not the green of spring
But green before the green, a spring before the spring –
A green deception in the hedge, lichen as heavy
On every branch and twig as if they had leafed already
To a green mist; and the ashy combings grass fades to
Drenched from the fields, and they at rest and bright, as new
Wet butterflies attune themselves on sunny stalks
Or women after childbirth in passive bloom relax –

Country still dreaming in the drag of the solstice, surely
It was a mirage day, whose sun shone late and early
Through winds of silk; and in the roadside's drift and brash
(Where the small fungus burns like seeds of fire in ash
And sleepless bramble plies all seasons over and under)
One green as strange as indoor light had pierced the winter –
Freak tongues of arum publishing so early, clamant,
Over our share of earth the undreamed-of spring ascendant.

A Past Generation

The people who were old when we were young,
Then this is where they were; who made no song
Of trials or sorrows, having still our nation's
Historic phlegm, having their generation's
Reserve, or call it their civility,
That would not hurt or embarrass needlessly:
The people who grew weak as we grew strong,
The old when we were young.

A Woman Condemned to Virtue

From future time the grey flowed into her hair
As the light flowed into her mirror from outer space.
She looked in the mirror and saw her mother there.

"It is only a trick of light, the snow in the air...
But how shall I live my life, wearing her face?"
From future time the grey flowed into her hair

While antique voices chimed how alike they were,
For words half heard may find their time and place:
She looked in the mirror and saw her mother there.

"But she stays home-bound, gentle and wise in her chair,
And I am the wild one that runs a dangerous race."
From future time the grey flowed into her hair,

And the impartial winter light laid bare
In the bones of her skull a genetic calm and grace.
She looked in the mirror and saw her mother there.

We range less far than we think and from anywhere
May round the world to a long relinquished base.
From future time the grey flowed into her hair:
She looked in the mirror and saw her mother there.

Waking Early

An over-pearled, a sunless morning: later, rain
Forecast, but now the season's plain
And long, long early hours;
Plain as a plain virgin's years
Spent in deeds of charity
(Flockings of birds imply, feeding from lawn and tree) –

Something I also love, unskilled to express its worth.
I wake on this known tract of earth,
Mankind asleep, but this
World at its domesticities
In the plain light, in the morning land;
And I a tourist here, to gaze, not understand.

A Present of Sea Shells

The shells are elaborate and curious
Like human thought, and yet not thoughts of ours.
A young boy searched them out on an island's shores
Where shells so perfect are not plentiful,
And in a carton, wrapped in cotton wool,
Sent them through air across the world to us,

Knowing that, settled far inland, we still
Love the sea's gifts, complex and beautiful.
This fact, this node of facts, in thought (like a shell
In the hand) I hold – the boy on the shore, the sun
On the wings of the mind-powered great machine homing in.
Time yields its patterned shells, none, none identical.

Waking in dark on the flat-lands of the night
To sadness, or space too vast, I light this light:
The boy designing our pleasure; and now, spread out
On a tray, the shells from their journeying. One is a dawn that
    pales,
One etched with finest fans on lapping scales,
One whorled; orange and green seem hand-strewn over it.

Views from a Train

First were fantastic clouds, visitings of wild sun,
Then over Shap the travellers, within
The cloud-scape as if journeying high by plane,

Became what they had seen, transfused to it.
But now the train, through level country lit
By evening moods, runs haltingly and late.

Where the enormous sun, white-golden, finally
Sets behind horizontal cloud like a sea
Its gold reflection dwells on that flood momentarily.

And colour pales, day's after-light takes over,
To shine from surfaces as black ice shines, wherever
Are offered to the sky canal or ox-bowed river;

To shine from wastes of metal strewn in yards
And broken windows of abandoned sheds;
To read our land with its blind hands before it fades.

The Unwritten Poem

The poem will not take its form, will not unravel,
However bright the leaves of chrome
And all the vinous reds hang from
The eaves in curtain-falls, or fallen tile the gravel,

However we may seem to walk like royalty
On richness, as the leaves disperse
And settling pattern earth and grass
And from themselves and us compose a harmony.

Though, treading leaves in this late month's luminous grace,
We gather certain days or hours
As if to fill a vase of flowers,
The poem will not take its form for all of this,

Knowing its concern is with what hardly can be told,
Not trusting to this fragile verse
The marriage and the distantness
Between the seeing mind and the envisioned world.

The Old Woman's Dream

She drowsed by day, being old: reality
Flowed into dream. And voices from nearby
Lawns, or of children loitering to play
On their route from the pool, these real voices came
Through the window and inhabited her dream.

For all that she knew clearly where she was
In her light sleep, still she wondered: are they ours –
Children's tones being so much alike – are those
Our children's voices? And her dreaming told
Her falsely, yes. A boy, say seven years old,

Come in by the glass door, sat briefly with her
And left, and came again with a girl. Together
In changing play they took one part and another –
Always her children. Nothing anywhere
Could be more natural than their being there.

Waking, she heard their voices ebb and drain
To those generic children in the lane
As colonists might be called home again;
And wondered, in the land from which they'd gone,
With what strange power the past claims to live on.

The Forester

He had left Burma the longest way, retreating
Northwards. He hardly ever spoke of it; rarely
Some fragment would out-crop – the rivers, the leeches –
A story told as interesting merely.

He had been a forester. When all was over,
The long march and the war, he awhile worked on
In other parts of the East – descendant of soldiers
And empire-builders in an empire gone.

But singular, not of any type. He would
Quote Milton and Gray to me. And once, long retired
(He told me) by chance on the other side of the world,
In Trinidad, walking on leaves he heard
And felt, smelt, tasted Burma – there young, complete,
Before he saw it was teak-fall at his feet.

Early Morning Overcast

1

This summer morning twilight without glory,
This light, condition of our seeing merely
And medium of being of all the living,

Limitless charity and clarification,
This light so softly advances that its motion
Seems a stillness abstracted from moving,

Seems a becoming without alteration;
As a ship watched, making harbour from the ocean,
Though it may be on some great arc curving

Yet rooted in our sight enlarges, flowering
A water-lily there – not, as in truth, nearing,
Shedding its wake and journey, arriving.

2

Light, visibility without glory.
No sign, no colour though the sun is risen surely.
Perfect and uniform the sky,
A wash of cloud, a willed opacity,

Pearled and translucent glass.
No colour but on earth. Long cords of flowers
The tall laburnum tree has loosed,
Summer-yellow, seem only to exist

For eyes; and yet will (not to over
Impress their beauty by pure stillness) waver
Lightly, and in civility
Answer the air and its endless pliancy.

Last night, a few hours past, the sun
Set so far to the north it caught in its shine
The highest branches and from there
Lifted into transcendence every twig and flower.

Gilder of gold, visible sun,
You waste your gifts doing what is already done,
Praising the proven beautiful.
Mere light, this morning without glory, can as well.

Three Poems in Memory of a Child

AN EARLY DEATH

Judith, my grandchild, older than I in death,
More learned in death than all the living, all
My parents' strong viable children, their
Children, and theirs: now in this seeming lull,
In the still, radiant autumn of this year,
Thinking of death, I think of you the more.

Love, I remember you twenty months old,
No toddler as a blonde child would have been –
A little girl, light running, a gazelle,
And gentle. I have not seen you since at all,
The Atlantic Ocean first, then death, between.
Of your long years you lived another one.

I called you learned in death more than us all,
Yet death you never knew in life, too young
Even to have heard its name, too quickly gone
For fear or pain to touch you, light gazelle.
And if the dead know death we cannot tell.
If in some way, in that way you know all.

226

And if in no way . . . yet to have been,
To have stood in the doorway in your shift of grace
With hands half lifted, so to have looked in
On mortal life, it is not nothing – is
A hammer stroke that rings and rings. Love, being
And not being both are strange; you belong to being.

THE NEW HOUSE

The new unfinished house
Had an emptiness, notwithstanding
The dusty garden soil
Brought in on feet or with winding
Of air through the window louvres,
And the florid heat abounding,
And the bell voices of children
Constantly sounding
Sweetly now, now clanging
Untimed; and with coming and going
The doors in the gusts banging.

The new inchoate house
Which the present and future filled
Had an emptiness, that held
The absence of the child,
The quiet one, never here.
And pain, unreconciled,
Drifting like air, dishevelled
The furnishing, and like stirring
Of earth had cracked the flooring:
Pain that can fracture the ground
Of a life beyond all curing.

This was before they had roofed
And walled with a lacy low
Parapet the verandah,
And planted quick to grow
Hibiscus, passion fruit,
And reclaimed the slope below
With pineapples and hardy

227

Root-crops and the rainfall tree.
This was while goats grazed free
Still over grass and thorns
And the litter of masonry.

But in those days, on the open
Verandah, work done, and cooled
The air and the thirsty land,
When the sun had dropped and the wild
Children had dropped like stones,
When they were still and were spread
Like wonders in shop windows
On the coverless sheet of the bed –
On the verandah, when light
From indoors fell soft as shade
And the voices of adults strayed,

Or the moon freed from the mountain
Poured equal light on the land,
The seaward fields and the sea's
Plains and long arc beyond –
On the sea and the unreclaimed
Land such quiet lay
As if the quiet child
Had taken her absence away;
Or as if the touch of the air
And the kindness of beauty and light
Had been news of her.

AN ISLAND GRAVEYARD

Wherever there are peopled islands there must be
Graveyards that overlook the sea.
They must be as numerous
As settled coasts; and the residuary grass
That snares our ankles will grow over
These wavy mounds and troughs everywhere, the survivo

Where the brute innocent vegetation that the sun
One month cuts down the next is grown,
Here upon this young child's stone

Incised, the lettering straggles slightly, that was done
by an inexperienced hand, and this
Falls like a grace or truth, almost a happiness;

Calling to mind her child's inaptitudes, her starts
Of learning and her unlearned arts
And all her moving ways, both those
That other children share and those uniquely hers;
Saying, her nature's lettering, that we
Hold carved in us, is tooled as well on history

And stored in history's silence. Not eternal life
But having lived pleads to my unbelief
Its claim to everlastingness.
No foothold seems for thought, nor comfort much in this.
The past endures under what sun?
But, that she lived (our love knows) cannot be undone.

Here on this skyward field where she is not, but where
We easily can speak of her,
Where eyes are filled with sea and air
A few trees spread, always in leaf, now bright in flower.
But, island child, the sea was hers.
The sea she loved be a wreath for her, beyond words or flowers.

The Witness

Master of life, if our kind
Of life must come to an end,
I say this not in despair
Nor protest but as being
A witness, who was there
And knows what he is saying:
There is gold in the sand,
I have held it in my hand.

229

Here marvels past pretence
Unfold, and innocence
From valleys where it keeps
Is evidenced to us.
The child in the cradle sleeps
A petal on the grass.
New on the frozen tree
Leaves answer human dignity.

And since we came our lives
Have fed your cosmos, leaves
Falling. What do you do,
Master of time, with the past
That is seamed through and through
With our known and unexpressed?
Such a strange, so rich, compost
Have you in mind to waste?

If our world is your mistake
All said, it is yours to unmake,
To end as you began it.
We are more dark than bright
Yet faint from our perished planet
Quenched here, an obdurate light
Of meaning and of grace
Would travel still through space.

The Coach to the Airport

I think of living children, recalling that journey:
Out of all possible children, those few or many
Caught by chance in the net of our world and century;

How one had slept with her head on my lap, from having
Been wakened too early that day, the day of their leaving –
She slept in the coach to the airport while either side
Mist filled the morning fields, and the boy astride
The arm of the seat exclaimed at the blind white vision
And the red sun rising, four times magnified –

And how these are two of the few (though to us they are many)
Out of possible beings, caught in our delicate prison,
Wild natures caught in the net of our world and century.

At the Airport

When their flight had been called and they had gone
After all suddenly out through the mean
Exit that seems a makeshift casual screen
And yet is mortal, one-way, absolute,
Having some time to waste before her return
She sat or wandered, empty of will and heart.

There, a boy stands at his group's circumference, one
Of those whose profile, as they turn the head,
Says, Nefrotete too had African blood.
There an old woman weeps as if alone –
Walled by strong presences and comforted
By loving words, as if for a death weeps on.

And carved in wood whether ash or ebony
Some merely wait, quite self-contained; yet wait
Filled with their purposes, the small or great.
The look of crowds is like the drift and stasis
Of leaves or birds in autumn; but reality
Here as with leaves and birds is meaning, crisis.

A View of Youth

These days, how ordinary beauty and well-being
And strength and competence themselves find speech and boast
In the young mature; and often, most unrealised, most.
And I recall half knowing this which now I am seeing.

Some of our gifts are given, some are briefly lent.
Theirs now an eloquence the cannot help nor hinder,
A marvellous fire and they the radiance of the tinder.
I thank them for its warmth, the meant and the unmeant.

Children Blowing Bubbles

Since they were told, not in the house,
Here in a public garden under trees,
Strangers come new to this classic childhood game,
Entranced they mime its ecstasies.

All is obedience. The gentle air
Follows the least variance of temperature
Unseen, unfelt. You would say there was no wind
But that the bubbles prove it there.

They map its hidden currents (who would guess
The lifts and falls and doublings of its course?)
They are that candle-flame or chemical
That brings the invisible writing out for us,

As poets ask their winding verse to be.
But children write their poems bodily.
Drawn after, they enact the rainbow globes
Their careful breath and hands set free:

Globes that hold images of sky and trees
Caught on their silvered journeying surfaces;
Children who run and dance to mirror these,
As pliant as the air, all instrument,
Patterning time like music with their fantasies.

Any Traveller's Apology

Part of my silence, part of my secrecy,
Was it a hard thing to ask you to be
Or the usual thing? This is obscure to me:
This clear: when in reality

Or fantasy I have been long away,
Say in the East or across the Ocean, say
Distant in work or mood from day to day,
Through being inescapably

The solitary traveller I am,
When I come home, to what but you do I come?
If you were gone I could never in fact or dream
Set out, for dread of coming home.

Two Sky Scenes

1

I saw the unformed reflection on a cloud
Shed upwards by the pure and early green
Of cloud-shaped trees; or rain it might have been
Hanging in clusters of green grapes before
The cloud, the vine-leaved porch, the lightning's door;

Or might have been a fluted pier of stone
In a grey-green cathedral, that the sun
Would analyse to a rainbow if it shone.
But neither sun nor lightning shone; the white
Blossom and leaves of earth shed all there was of light.

2

The sky is almost clear. A sole star shows,
Another, then another, through the salmon-rose
False dawn the city lights all night compose
Out of their sulphur and their snow's
White beyond roofs. Elsewhere the moon is in its third

Quarter, obtuse. And obliquely a strange cloud
Flows by, ghost-like though shaped as a blade.
But the moon imposes its nature's solitude.
No cloud comes near it ever, only seems
It does, like the events of dreams.

A Leave-Taking

He went away early. He was not tired
But he was young, foreign too, his hosts were old
And the boundaries of communication had
Loomed frowning, most was told that could be told,

Affection, happiness were verified.
It was they who might be tired. He said goodbye
As if in a flowering hedge his hand had stayed
On a wicket gate, going out regretfully.

And by his tact subduing diffidence
The boundaries of communication shone
Changed to a line of light, as all at once
Past darkening roofs the distant street lamps are turned on.

The Coat

Strange sadness can assail one:
This woman saw from the house
Past ferns and an azalea
And shifting leaves of trees
Her husband stooped at weeding,
His coat the colour of dark
Blue-black duffel fading
Moving and bent to work;
And, hands in water, thought,
Weighing her liberties,
I will finish and go out –
Then heard his voice indoors,

And whirled in a circle, saw
Past the deceit of leaves
What had seemed his coat before
Had become the dusk of caves
Rose and forsythia fashion
Arched over in their season:
Mere shadow and recession,
And sadness loosed from reason.

A Day in Childhood

Then when I stayed with my friend in the South
The lanes flowered early in the year. It seems
I had never seen before growing wild on earth

White among purple violets, all but thatched over
By winter grass at the hedge roots, and their own
Unfolded nesting leaves as well for cover.

She chose the purple, I the white.
The white reflected purple, now I see,
And those seem pale, by darkness drained, or light.

So now I imagine as I recall them
Abundant then in the hedges of the South,
Coiled, scentless, tender, infantinely small.

Now I interpret, then I knew
Only a wondering bliss, and could not tell
When homesickness, being unattended to,

Was lifted; but recall how down the lane
Long with its many windings, in untroubled pleasure
We bowled our hoops, safely, as you could then.

Water Images

THE TIDAL RIVER

The trees descend, image of love,
To drink the brackish water of
Estuary or tidal river,
To lean their inland fulness over
That bright and far-brought mineral other.

THE STREAM

So turbid though I am,
Rooted in me the young
Floated like water lilies –
That now alight like swans.

THE WELL

The stone you let fall in me will not resile
Nor echo nor give any sign awhile.
Wait for my word. A lifetime you may wait,
I am so deep, my depth so obdurate,
Not with my will but through my fate.

Cut Tulips

Cut tulips, red and white,
    forming of themselves a glass,
Drafting on air the bowl of a wine-glass
    over the straight stem of their vase,
They are infallible to eyes
    as are the beautiful young
Who in their bodies' bearing
    and movement can do nothing wrong,
Who never needed learn
    grace of deportment; nor need these,

Whether as now they mime a glass
  or curve to window-gaze;
While shaped as a fostering calyx, from
  the base of each petal rose-
Red or a muted crimson the colour
  spreads, to seem it flows
Out to the white border, there
  arrested at its perfect moment stays.

Ghosts Not Seen

Possibly you are right to feel afraid.
It may be earth is haunted everywhere,
Every least space, every foot of ground or floor.
And your slow walk at times may tell you wade
Through seas of ghosts not seen – waylaid, waylaid –

As some dark woman through her zone's encumbering air
Slowly, respectful of heat, paces its ocean-bed
(The mangoes ripening in the basket on her head) –

But you, like me, see no ghosts so you fear.
Those who see ghosts, they say, are not afraid.

Grammarian's Hymn

Sum, es, est.
Loved of all verbs best,
Esse, the most pervasive;
Though quietest, recessive
When in words of love or praise
Sum is dissolved in *es*,
Or *est* itself may drown
In the ocean of its noun
As Buddhist saints are given
To their subsuming heaven.

Esse, auxiliary,
A servant, ancillary,
Passed over, tangential,
Factotum, essential,
Invisible, implied
As air is far and wide
And even beyond, in space
(Abating mind's distress)
Fulfilling emptiness.

A Choice

There are other doors
Out of any dream. Someone
In me chose waking.

Pigeons in Early Light

Two, in the grey of dawn, the large birds are
Settled in plum-tree branches deep in flower
A knight's move from my window here.

Another, full of its business, has flown
High up into a pine and walks upon
A horizontal branch, half-seen

Through the clustered quills. The two in the plum-tree sit
Among white flowering twigs like native fruit,
Close though a little separate.

I could not tell at first what kind of bird
Made dusk in the unborn day – until one reared
Its beautiful small serpent head

Weaving in air, on the too fine neck above
The cumbered heavy weight of the emblem dove;
And made its single tree a grove –

Where three birds house, now the other has flown down.
They are grouped for their reasons so, in the worlds they own.
Their worlds seem grouped like stars in mine.

Reflecting on Old Age

We are as light as wood ash, dense as stone.
Our muscles come to know the weight of bone,
The sensual happiness of lying down.
A little milk the gradual years have pressed
Into our eyes that easily over-run.
Our vague hair is as volatile as dust.

Waking and sleep are mutual, so far on
In marriage that we speak of one alone,
Sleep without waking, as in a foreign tongue
Stumbling on consonants. Against the dark,
Coeval kindness, beneficence of the young
With our time's cares cross in a lattice-work.

Honey of small events, of passing states
We take – as when a light flame oscillates
In the smokeless coal. In the winter grate's
Rock garden it blows, translucent as a wild
Flower, as woodsorrel; or a bird's heart, it beats;
And gives peace, as if worlds were reconciled.

On the railway bank not only bracken, once,
I remember, but the dying grass was bronze
In transverse light; and beyond the journey, friends.
Happiness even passing imagination,
Foretold by straws of grass and bracken fronds,
Late in the day, their welcome at the station.

Too hard in age to trawl the heavy seas.
I settle for summations, instances,
Remembering (in time's interstices)
Time taken to sit in the tropic after-sun
In an open gallery, in hands cup or glass,
With two or three; here now, by a fire, with one.

Thanks for a Present

A silk scarf: feel of air, colour of space.
The smaller bring the larger things to mind,
As often; as in a mirror's frame and glass
The un-blown curtain's fall, the tree beyond –
Liana-patterned fall, the pine tree's down-
Sweep as of arms, and up-held fingers where
Its cones nest (but the birds nest further in,
Magpie or dove, seen or imagined there) –
All these, the mirror's frame and twice-born light,
Receiving, turn to strange. So, mirrored in
The scarf you gave me – like a cloud to sight,
Like air to touch – I have been given again
(Besides itself, for which I thank you most)
These other gifts, that for a time I had lost.

A Landscape with a Woman and Child

On the flowing ground once quarried for limestone,
Once coral under sea, the soil now is thin
And sparely grassed and flowered with eyebright, carline
Thistle, centaury; with gentians, the one
That grows two inches tall, a sapphire candle.
Scattered or grouped, these on their complex terrain
As wavy as seas, first hardly visible
Then one by one, then many, make themselves seen.

The young woman from breast to shoulder lifts
The baby, just skilled to balance his heavy head
And gaze on this new walk over hillocks and troughs
Out of eyes blue with infancy. When now instead
He closes these, they also are little hills,
Moated by gentler slopes; light shadows flower their dales.